Dark Night
and
Brighter Days

Kent Berry

To order additional copies of this book, contact:
Xlibris Corporation
1-888-795-4274
www.Xlibris.com
Orders@Xlibris.com
84924

To my Mother Frances E. Berry, who taught me
the meaning of Unconditional Love

Contents

PART II

An old man's winter evening

Snowflakes race in spiral lines
to gather on the laden pines
that humbly bow beneath the strain
of heavy snow and frozen rain.

Now and then a branch will break
beneath the uninvited weight
and is buried in a grave of snow
no one but I will ever know.

Though the path to Ison's place
has for the moment been erased
I think that I shall always know
the way that is the best to go
with memories from so long ago.

There she lays, ole Ison's pond
the one we used to gather on
where I'd bust my butt and bruise my head
and push and pull that wooden sled
that papa let us help him make
that time it snowed on Christmas day.

Faintly now I think I hear
the sound of children's laughter near
and I become a child again
playing here with all my friends.

Over the hill comes a bundled bunch
I'm not real sure but I have a hunch
that's old man Ison's great grandkids
came home for Christmas like I did.

They came to play; I came to sleep
for now the snow is far too deep
and thoughts are heavy on me now
that make my wearied head to bow.

For soon I know they'll carry me
with all my friends and family
down the isle and through the gate
to my plot at Aldersgate.

They'll bid me bye; They'll bid me well;
of after-life though; who can tell?

In the end I bend for fear I'll be
A stone in the mist of stones
A name in a field of names
and who will ever know, but me?

kent

Arkansaw

Arkansaw had a banjo.
He played it every night
we'd all listen to Arkansaw
and forget The War for a minute
some turned their heads to cry.

He never mentioned her by name
but he nursed a broken heart
called her names like darlin and sugar and honey
we could tell that she must of been something special
by the way he played and sang.

The War was a small thing for Arkansaw
he had bigger battles to fight
half the time he'd misplace his balls
or get his powder wet
but he wouldn't part with that banjo
come hell or high water
he'd hold it above his head.

Ole Arkansaw had a banjo
he could pick it to a fair thee well
we all placed bets on what her name was
but Arkansaw wouldn't tell.

BAYOU METO

Words are thoughts incarnate
ideas manifest
the liquid side of vapor
condensated into flesh.

Like the water that rest in the bayou
because the slope of the land is flat.
The water lays quiet and still and placid
and sometimes, I like to think, asleep.

But when the rain comes
and the water awakens and starts to run
sometimes the flow is swift
and the level rises up to the brim and then
over the bank.

Such running water everywhere
that one can hardly scoop it up
and most of it slips away.

And the water rises higher, up to the horses bridal
and hope begins to swell, that the horse too can swim.
But even a horse as good as he
can't swim indefinitely
with me up high on him.

I get down to wade with him
and we walk gingerly through the murky water
he shakes his mane and gives a brisk snort
as if to complain or maybe explain
we're both in this together.

The water slips down the bayou
and out to the river and down to the sea
and eventually up to the sky, even above the sky;
The firmament.

You can't always see it there
but it's there
waiting to return to me.

And when it returns
I like to turn my face upward
and open my mouth
and catch the remnants
that are lured to me.

Who could complain?
What mysteries explained!
The wonder and comfort,
recycled rain.

BIG BROTHER

Everyone needs a good poem
Who could disagree?
So the Bureau of Standards in Agreement
      of what we all doth need.
Established a law; all by themselves.

The law read thusly: This is the way that it shall be.
To everyone who hath no poem
      a poem shall be freely given; and likewise inverted
To everyone who hath more than one poem
      poems shall be freely taken.

And everyone agreed in agreement
This law was surely good,
      mostly because it felt that way.

So by coercion they took poems
      from the more fortunate, the lucky, the poets
      and from all of those who where blessed by whatever
      gods there be, to have and to hold, to feel and to know,
      poems.

The Poem Police were ruthless.
They took poem after poem by force
until the poets were poor
in sprit and in truth
Saying: what is the use?
      of tilling and hoeing
      of raking and sowing
of struggling by the sweat of the brow, to reap
just to have it taken away; and unappreciated at that.

The takers allocated
      while the bureaus produced bureaus.
And everybody reported to somebody,
The Poem Police reported to:

The bureau of the Poem Police
who reported to The bureau of   Oversight
who reported to The bureau of   Language Use
who reported to The bureau of   Investigation
who reported to The bureau of   Common Unity
who reported to The bureau of   Everything
who themselves, as a public manifestation
     of their ethical propriety, graciously
     reported to The Bureau of Standards in Agreement.
Therefore everybody knew that all was fair and just.

But, there was one big problem.
Perfectly good poems were spilt, ruined
     and simple lost all along the way.
And the lazy wanted more free poems
     and they treated the poets with contempt.
And the poets grew weary, tired, and frustrated.
Saying: Poems should be exempt!

Times got so bad that one couldn't even push one
perfectly good poem down the bureau chain
to it's rightful owner, the needy.
Before the poem would get even halfway down the chain
It would completely vanish, gone into thin air.
It simply ceased to exist, evaporated.
No level of accounting could account for it.
It was gone. That is all that anybody knew.
          And everybody knew that.
The lazy began using poems as floor mats.
The poets hid them in their cupboards
The children grew spiritually skinny, physically fat,
     without form and void
     wanting only affirmation
     idle, hour upon hour.
The poets lost hope.
The lazy bellyached.
The bureaus begat bureaus.
And Life was; As Life is.

kent

BEAUTY

Yes it is true; beauty is in the eye of the beholder, just look and see.
Sometimes it may be the way a mother holds her baby,
Or maybe how a mother bird feeds her baby bird
Or a young tender blossoming flower
Or someone's heartfelt laughter
Or a delicate thin cloud
a big tall oak tree
a little bee
& one day
maybe
me.

BE CAREFUL

You
be careful
in whose hands
you put your heart.
Some people are clumsy,
and they break things.
Things that they
can't begin to
replace.
kent

BELIEFS

The life he lived
didn't match what he believed
rather than change his life
he simply changed his beliefs.

bIg

She was BIG and pregnant,
pleasantly plump.
She ran a bath,
in that claw-foot tub
and quickly sunk,
beneath the bubbles,
her belly stood up.

With an angelic voice
she began to sing:
"Momma's little baby
loves shortnin' shortnin' . . .
momma's little baby
loves shortnin' bread."

We never dreamed,
in all the dreams we dreamed,
that momma's little baby,
would be born dead.

BITTERSWEET

Beneath the moon
Beside the sea
Her moistened lips they beckoned me
and bid me there to take the bait
but avoid the snare.

The precious fruit
the glimmering hook
the road to heaven,
the path I took.

Entangled in her heart and arms,
the bonds that bound me on the beach,
the grasp beyond my feeble reach,

the lies that bid me
to take her there
turned bittersweet
upon my tongue,
and in my heart.

CIVIL WAR SOLDIER

I wonder what a civil war soldier would think
if he were to come back to this world
and looked around to see, what became of all that fightin'.

He would see cities sprouted up
like mushroom on little piles of dung called towns.
Big highways made of hard stuff where trails were that he
had rode.

He would see:
People leaving their homes on weekends,
(Homes with running water, hot and cold
and in-house out-houses, and wired for fire.)
just to live in tents beside the lake.

I'm sure he would be curious
I'm hoping not furious
I doubt he'd think it was worth it.

COLD NIGHT

The daytime faded into another lonesome night.
There were no channels which interested me.
No book could hold my attention.
They all felt like the night air - cold.

I searched on line for something to do;
something to learn, to feel, to know.
But nothing could hold my attention.
I walked outside beside the lake
and tried to think,
but the cold wind
chased me back in,
back inside to pace.

I knew I could drink but I didn't want to.
Even that had no luster this night.
Then, out of nowhere
she calls me on the phone.
I was glad to hear her voice.
Glad that she would be able to hear
for herself that my speech wasn't slurred.

She said she just called
to see if I would answer the phone.
I have no idea what that meant.

She said she had to run,
but that she was going to call me right back.
She asked me if I would answer again.
I told her of course I would.

I hung up the phone.
It never rang again.
The cold went clear to my bones,
and stayed there.

COLD DARK RAIN

That's okay my baby
you go on and cry
I can't no more make you happy
can't no more satisfy
than I can stop this pouring rain
- it hurts to see you cry
I can't identify
what you want.
Dressings are clean
food to spare
Not too hot nor cold
No pinches nowhere.
What's wrong my pretty baby?
Please don't cry
been up half the night.
Go ahead and cry your heart out
if that's the way you want it.
Go ahead and cry my baby.
I can no more stop this rain
Than I can find out what is wrong for you
and see you satisfied.
Hush, Hush My Child
I've got to go to work now
I've got to get out in that rain
But I'll be thinking about you.
You go ahead and cry
-if that's the way you want it.
I can't satisfy.
I'll be thinking about you
I'll be crying there with you
-in this cold-dark pouring rain.

COLD

The rain feel soft
and clung as ice
to every branch, twig
or soul in sight.

COMMUNICATION

Communication.
I should have majored in communication.
If the most important thing in life is relationships,
than the next most important thing would be,
communication.

I don't communicate very well.
I find myself signing on to little battles,
when quite frankly, I don't even like to fight.

Even if I did, these little battles are so piss-ant,
so small,
even if I won, it wouldn't mean a hill of beans.

And they eat up my time
which is to say, the stuff of life.
They eat up my life.
As does all strife, and friction.

The engine wears out because of friction.

I don't want to fight.
I want to live and love and laugh.
Not all the time,
but most of the time.

I can't seem to get that across.
As time slips to loss.
And the pounding pummels my head.
In a moment we'll all be dead.
Let's don't fight.

Forgive me now my trespasses,
and if ye owe me any, then I forgive thee.

Would that I could communicate
and lay my burdens down
and watch the sunsets with wonder
with someone like⸺.

COMMUNION

Jesus loves you
Sister so-and-so just said,
I thought unto myself
I'm oh so glad he did.

For what if Jesus hated me?
And all my children dead
not only just my firstborn
but all of them instead.

And all of me would be skinless
not only just my heart.
And everyone would misunderstand
not just the ones that count.

If Jesus didn't love me,
I'd be drawn and quartered
in the marketplace, bankrupt
for all the world to see.

She said that Jesus loved me.
I just smiled and said He did.
She smiled back like a lobotomized chimpanzee.
As I took the sacrament.

CORNBREAD

Cornbread dropped back
And let that axe head fly.
With a strong hard thump,
the axe head hit.
The big stump split.

Then Cornbread let out
a deep chested shout:
"Let there be no doubt,
I's from That Big Balled
African Tribe."

CURIOUS GROUP

It is a curious group
they shuffle in just past noon
each Sunday.
They are dressed nice enough
and their hair is fixed all pretty
and their appetites are large enough.
They like to eat.
But their conversations are curious.
I know that a few hours ago
they were talking about love and forgiveness
talking about grace, redemption, salvation.
But now here at the Shoppe
they talk about a weaker member
as though he need be cut off from the herd
as if he were in league with Satan.
These Christians are a curious race.
I know of no other place
where they castigate the weaker ones
and then devours them like rabid cannibals.

Dear Mom,

Do come down and see me.
You'll find the District there is fun.
The Main Library is a stones throw there
and there is a wonderful little book store
right across from Sticky Fingerz.

We can even stroll on down to Clinton's Library.
Remember when I introduced Him to You in Redfield?
Remember how you were never going to wash that hand
because the Gov'ner had shook it?

Time has a way of changing things.
Everything but us.

We can go any where we want to.
We can do whatever we want to too.
Or, we can just sit and chit and chat and smile.
Do come down and see me there.
I can find you a place to park.

I think it would do us good.
Let's get out for a little while.

kent

DICHOTOMY

My grandfather
on my father's side
was an amiable alcoholic.

My grandfather
on my mother's side
was an amiable preacher.

I
on my mother's
and father's side
am all Gemini.

Split between the middle
from head to toe
torn in both directions
is all I've ever known.

DON'T KNOW WHY

I've been around the block
no less than a time or two.
I've been tired and weak
from the endless strain and let go
when perhaps I should have held on to.

I've watch the sun set alone
miles from any home
and felt the cold wind
deep inside my bones
as sleep teased
but shied away from me.

I've stood beside my first-born's grave
and cursed God for not doing something
when doing something was so easily within his reach.
At times I've tried to make amends with God
though I don't know why, I don't know why.
For if He is neither impotent, nor benign
what kind of God have I ?

FAIRY TALES

Fond took a liking to Like
Like was down for anything
So they both hooked up
On a misty night

Like and Fond,
they hit it off just right.
Together they begat Love
and lived happily ever after.

FAMILY

I've been thinking about my family a lot lately.
I'm not sure why, maybe just age.
My thoughts run the full spectrum,
Mom to Dad-
my own children, to siblings
from the youngest to the oldest
those living
those dead
the rights (trust me, there are many)
the wrongs (they stand out because they are strange)
The nieces, the nephews
the balanced
the extremed.
Aunts and Uncles-
all those in between.

It is hard to believe, but I believe it is true.
None of us are in prison.
Mother was right . . .
there is a God.

FEAST FOR A WEEK

Because I learned to read;
I feasted for a week.

It started with Melville's "Moby Dick."
I myself was Captain Ahab as
I sought that big white beast,
as the hounds from hell, they hounded me.
I swore by whatever gods might be.
that I would not die, I would not rest,
until I'd found and bound that great white fish.
I found her, but she bound me
and I died bound against her ruthless breast.
This I did early on the first day.

For desert I chomped on a little bit of Chomsky
I can only eat him in little bits,
lest my head hurts and the digestion is slow.
When the food is rich, best you bite in bits.

Later that evening, when my work was done
I had a meal with Stevenson, Robert Louis that is.
And I became a man who was altogether me, better yet . . .
altogether we.
For I was myself encased as one, "Dr. Jeckle and Mr. Hyde".
These I knew from being a Gemini: I could relate from every side.
And loved the darkness, while loving light, and loathed the split
tight heart inside.
I was sadly glad when I finally died, no more darkness, no more
light.
After that I went to sleep, pondering my day.

The second day was no less a joy
I leapt out of bed a little boy and made my way to the library.
There were so many choices which I could make, from Dante's "Inferno",
to Emerson's "Walden", or Steven Crane's "Red Badge of Courage", The list goes on and on.
I settled for a struggle; "The Grapes of Wrath."
Steinbeck and I, and a host of cast, set off out west without looking back.
We had dust for breakfast, sand for dessert,
as we went searching for that American Dream. The trip was harsh, the earth was mean. Flesh and dust and the in between.
While I enjoyed Steinbeck's company, his rich vocabulary stimulated me,
I was oh so glad to get back home.
I took a bubble bath, listened to Stravinsky's "Rite of Spring."
and promptly took a break.

I skipped lunch from being full.
And took a stroll beside the lake
The moon was full in the broad of day.
I thought of Frost's "North of Boston".
I tucked whatever thoughts away
and saved them for another day,
knowing how way leads on to way.

Later that evening, the second day
I picked up a woman, what a woman indeed!
We embraced all evening, intertwined our minds.
As "Atlas Shrugged" I loved Ayn Rand.
Dapneye Taggart took on the Establishment as
a "Don Quixote" takes on windmills. Except her mills were real.
She filleted weak men like fish and stood her ground.
She was easy to love, I couldn't put here down.
The morning and evening was the second day.

The third day after a restful night
I meditated on my mind, wondering what to feed it.
I knew it needed nourishment as I felt a longing for content.
My mind needed meat. I took a look at Dale Carnegie.
"How to Win Friends and Influence People" I started for breakfast
and continued for lunch, later that night I gave it a try.
I made friends with the world and the world was friends with me.
If I wanted a smile, I had but to smile. If I wanted to be happy,
I had only to act happy and soon happy I would be.
What a marvelous discovery, so simple, complete,
all because I learned to love to read.
That morning and the evening was the third day;
the third day of a feast for a week.

The next day at the crack of dawn
I got up and going. I had awakened to a brand new world.
The birds were signing, the sunshine friendly, the wind refreshing;
I started to skip down the sidewalk and I saw people smiling
whom I couldn't
recall ever having seen them smile before. I was having an
influence, just as the book said, and the influence was good,
just like Mr. Carnegie had said. What could be better than this?
An adventure; I said.
So I picked up a book and went on a trip. I went with Jules
Verne, "Twenty Thousand Leagues Under the Sea".
What a trip I took beneath the sea! The scientist I meet taught
me so much. Things I had never thought of,
things that I didn't know that I didn't know, he explained with a
language that made perfect sense to me.
The landscape beneath the water was so vivid and lovely as
any mountain above,
with fishes and dolphins and all manner of life, the ocean was
teaming with life, and so was I.
When I returned my head was light and my legs were wobbly,
unaccustomed to solid ground.

But after a minute or two I was back to myself and I slid back
home waving at new friends along the way.
That was day four, of my feast for a week.
Just think what I would have missed, if I hadn't learned how to
read.

I took the fifth day as a precious jewel.
Just like it was when I was in school; for I was learning, but my
week was over half way over,
five sevenths to be exact. I wanted to savor each morsel of life.
I thought of tasty, good food for the soul.
And settled for King Solomon, the wisest of men I am told.
A little sleep, a little slumber, a little folding of the hands.
In all thy ways acknowledge Him, and He shall direct thy paths.
This took the hassle from planning
so far in advance.
This I learned on the fifth day,
then slept a sweet sleep.

The sixth day, my first thought, the last day of work
the next day for rest.
So I righted my mind, focused on work that was good
and choose to spend my day
with the father of American literature.
Oh, it wasn't Faulkner nor the great Hemingway.
The father, in my opinion, is none other than Mark Twain.
So we bummed and piddled around in a familiar place
Hannibal was as home to every Southern State
situated on a river, a mighty one at that. The days were arduous
The night's placid, and the people were human,
on each and every page. "The Adventures of Huckelberry Finn"
Me and my good luck, spent a whole day with Huck, and Jim,
we feasted on Southern
then called it a day. Day number six. The last day for work.

On the seventh, On the Sabbath,
I did not leave my house.
I did not leave my home.
I did not work.
I did not cook.
I read The Good Book
starting at the first.

I did not find it hard to believe
that I was made from mud.
But in all honesty I doubted that the whole universe's "Genesis"
was completed in just one week.
But so much of what I read was like a book of me.
The struggle between good and evil.
The blackness of my heart.
The comfort that comes from faith,
was quite a "Revelation" to me.
Before I faded to sleep, I was humbly thankful
that even if my mind was made from mud
I was thankful that it could read.
Thankful for a steady diet, for never having known true hunger.
Thankful for my feast of a week.
Thankful that I'd learned to love.
Thankful that I had learned to read.

FIRE AND ICE

Sunshine dances on sickles of ice
Shimmering glimmering glittering light
See the light Waltzing; beautiful sight
Twisting and Turning; resembles a fire
Crescendo then Nothing; hope and desire

Your love and my loneliness
I never could tire;
Of longing for your loveliness
The ice and the fire.

FIRST MATE MESS

It is hard to sail this dingy boat
on choppy seas.
My first mate and I speak different languages.
We come from the same small state
but cannot even communicate.

I'm thinking about water rushing in
on starboard side and the fate of going down, down, down.
I ask in simple English:
Honey, could you fetch me a pail so I can bail, a little water.
But all she hears, I swear I think she hears, is:

Did you see the mate that guy had back at Bimini?
Did you see how she moored that Rig?
Did you see her tie that bowline knot?
And pulled the sheets all nice and taut?
Man that guy's girl was nice and hot.

As I'm waiting for the pail,
She hurls it for my head.
And the water keeps rushing in.

Forgiveness

If I lost it all last year
because she had been unfaithful
and found comfort in another man
I could forgive that swiftly
without bonds of memory
It would be an easy thing to do.

And if I lost it all
because of something she thought
if she really thought
that I had been untrue
for as wrong as her strong
suspicions might be
I know I could forgive that too.

But if I lost it all
because she lost confidence
in the dreams that I pursued
then forgiveness comes harder
for I'm such a good starter
but poor on my follow through.

FREUDIAN

I think I have been guilty of using the word -friend- too loosely.
Or maybe I just see what I want to see.
Maybe instead of Freudian slips,
- I have Freudian sees.

Have you ever had a Freudian hear?
Or witnessed someone who swore they heard
something that wasn't said; something that could not be.
Rather than think them a liar,
I extend to them the benefit of the doubt.
(a weakness that I tout)
It may have merely been a Freudian hear.

Just,
a pigment of the imagination,
a marring of the mind,
a function of the brain.

Friends

Twiddle de dee
and Twiddle de dumb
sat on the bank
drinking some rum.

Twiddle de dee got up
and skipped a rock
clear across the lake
then said,
look what I done done.

Twiddle de dumb stood up
said, so what? watch this.
Skipped a rock
off de dee's head.

But Twiddle de dee
didn't think it funny
and he didn't like no more
no Twiddle de dumb.

FRUIT

There really isn't any more use in pretending
that we have a problem with color;
we don't have a problem with color,
we have a problem with fruit.
I hope that doesn't sound cowardly.

The problems are the result
of suspicion and predispositions
from DNA gone back,
way back;
from generation, to generation, to generation,
all the way back to just a few first people.
We are talking thousands and thousands,
of years,
of earthly years.

A very long time, in and by OUR time; but
a nanosecond in COSMIC time.

One man's ancestors bore the brunt
of the labor
without pay
without compensation
only fear of the lash.

But the law of compensation
has a way of leveling things out.
So any man with these genes
can walk and work in confidence
of reaching for The Dream,
Fulfillment is inevitable
It's laden in the genes.

Another man's fathers
struggled under the yoke
of providing
getting wares to the marketplace,
connecting maker with desire
and hopefully picking up a living
teaching his children along the way.
With a jaundiced eye I say;
The noblest of men to me.

Another man's ancestor
learned the strut,
learned how to march in order,
property of the state.
With stately plans and orders,
passed along within his genes.

Each man's heritage inevitable and invariably
goes back to somewhere,
to any and to all degrees.
We all fall somewhere.
We fall upon our birth.

So to judge a man on his skin color is foolish.
No man is Black: No man is White.
All skin colors are somewhere in between.
The closest to black, I've ever seen
was a man named Idi Amin.
But even he shouldn't be judge by his skin color.
He should be judged by his fruit;
as we all shall,
as we all are.

Are we not commanded?:
"You shall know them by their fruit"
And another,
"who by reason of use of your senses
have determined between good and evil".

It is good to judge fruit.
It is a major function of the brain.
But to judge the fruit, by looking at the color of a man's skin
is not judgment at all, it is pure ignorance,
in full bloom, for all the world to see.

Some men bare good fruit,
some men bare bad.
It isn't the color of the skin that means,
what kind of fruit he brings.
It has more to do with upbringing.

Good fruit needs good nourishment
It needs sunshine, and sometimes grafting
which makes the tree weep.

Good fruit is what I long for
Good fruit is what I seek
It has nothing to do with my color
I suspect it is in my genes.

Jesse's Girl

I'd like to have a girl like Jesse James had,
who when I said let's saddle up
didn't just stand there and ask;
where are we going and why?
And then stand there and say that that was too far
and tell me there were Pinkerton agents all over
the place
and tell me they have one of them fancy time-clocked
safes.

I'd like a girl who when I said, let's saddle up!
Went and put my favorite saddle on White Lightning.
And after I'd mounted first
then she'd jump on that horse
and ride with me.

To the ends of the world if need be;
arms round my waist,
cheek on my back,
now and then she'd squeeze me tight,
and take in a deep scent,
as if I was the most wonderful thing in the world,
as if I were, Jesse James.

And if I asked her why she didn't ask me where we
were going,
she'd say it didn't matter as long as I was there
and she was there
and we were together.

I like to dream a lot.
After all, it is my dream
and I can dream it like I want to.
I'll have a girl like Jesse had.

GLIMPSES

Sunshine now has gone away
Nighttime last for days and days
Now and then a ray breaks through
Memories of my stronger youth

HERE THERE AND IN BETWEEN

The huge plough ploughs the ground
The big ship ships everything
The little car carries me
and my bumper bumps
all kinds of things.

I DON'T WANT MY CHILDREN TO SEE

I don't want my children to see
some parts of me.
I scoop up piles of trash
from out my truck
discarded sandwich wraps
and cups, and more cups
some turnt on there sides
that spill coffee
or coke syrup
onto the carpet.
That is all fine by me.
It is only a truck
and I am only me.
But for some natural
perfectly explainable reason
I don't want my children to see.

The Road Taken

We, mankind I mean
Were not content to let the road
Lay gentle against her crest and down her lap
We'd rather the road run through her heart.

So with blasting caps and dynamite
We took by force what she wouldn't cede
And pounded hard against her chest
And scraped big chunks of sedimentary flesh

Inch by inch and day by day
We worked our way down to the base
To where we'd rather our road to lay
And paved it tight and made it bend
All smoothed out, and blended in.

We had our way with her against her will
We threw the view we had away
And left our children as an inheritance
An asphalt road and a carved up breast.

kent

I REMEMBER

Wow!
It is hard to think,
that my baby girl,
would be turning twenty!
The big two-o.

I was to be her protector.
I was to watch her grow!
I knew she would not be perfect
because I knew her mother,
because I knew me too.

She had her mother's beautiful lips
and she had my father's finger nails
though her's were tiny and shiny
they were shaped like his,
exactly the same.

You could see her mother
in those sparkling blue eyes;
her precious, prescient smile.
I know, because
I **did** watch her grow,
I watched her every week.
I doubt I missed a one.

I remember her as a child
wanting to eat dirt,
I suspect she got that from me.
But when she wanted to run around naked,
well, there is no suspecting,
she got that from me too.

I remember her missing teeth
and her feeling awkward;
the awkwardness that comes
from being a girl.
Things that I don't know.

I remember those horse back rides
with her flopping curly hair.
I remember the sun soaked canoe trips.
I remember her laughing so hard
that she pee'd her pants.
I couldn't let her live it down.
I remember wanting to shoot that boy,
who came a calling, all nervous and stiff.

I remember the hugs,
I remember the cries,
I remember how it might have been,
if my little Emma,
my precious Emma,
had never died

I RISE

Like the phoenix from the ashes rose
I rise.
Like the oak tree from the acorn grows
I rise.
Like the rising tide rolls
I rise.
Like the only Son arose
I rise.
Like the morning sun aglow
I rise.
Like the phoenix from the ashes rose!
I rise.
I Rise.
I RISE!

I SAW JESUS TODAY

I saw Jesus today
I was turning right on High Street
It is right past Rock Street
which is just past Battery
(I wonder why we don't have an Assault Street)
But I was going to say
I saw Jesus today.
He was right there in the sky.
Two big tall billowing clouds had parted
and the Sun was shining through
The Son was right there in the middle
I wished I had had a camera
He was standing there with his out stretched arms
his beard and robe were perfect.
I imagined that I heard him say:
"Come unto me all ye that labor
and are heavy laden and I will give you rest."
That sounded good.
I could use some rest.
But I had errands to run . . .
I had to get to Sam's and buy some plates
and Orange Juice and biscuits and things.
I headed right on High
and merged onto I-630.
I looked into my rearview mirror
the clouds parted and He was gone.

LAUNDRY

Whenever I do laundry
I'm oh so politically correct.
I ain't one to segregate,
and do one with hot
while leaving another one cold.

They are all just clothes.
Who is someone else to tell me
the proper way to do coloreds?

I do them all the same.
I'm enlightened!
I know the truth!
Let them all fade,
into one big glorious beige.

LAWYERLY

I had dropped a lease agreement off
for my lawyer to peruse before I signed.
I was chatting with the clerk out front
when through the door
a young man walked in.

He was dressed to the nines
in an expensive suit
which really didn't suit him well . . . at all.
I'm no fashion critic
(anyone who knows me can vouch for me on that)
but I can spot a suit too big.

"Well look at you boy
You clean up well
In fact you look . . . . lawyerly."

Well, Thank-you! he said.
He was sincere.
I was too.

Who but a lawyer
could interpret such an insult,
as the highest of compliments?

LITTLER

Except you become
as a little child.
When I was a little boy
even littler than I am now
I was full of great ideas
always fixing big problems
with simple answers,
simple for me that is.
For example: On poverty,
If I was in charge,
I would simply crank up them printing presses
Crank out ten thousand dollars for each poor person to have.
Wallah! No more poor people . . . . Next Problem Please!
Nuclear War: No Problem.
Since it was mostly them Russkies and US
We could draw sides, Each nation could choose
and join in the effort for its respective choice.
(Remember the key word here is choice;
Freedom was imperative from my perspective.)
Then we could engage in one big conflict,
with snowballs this time.
Three snowballs to each man,
not too hard of snowballs
lest you put out an eye.
The winner would be the one who tagged the other's leader
if that leader wasn't Safe, wasn't on Base.
Next Problem Please!
It was an easier time then
when I was littler and all.
Or maybe my thinking was clearer then,
not burdens by all these distractions,
obscured by light refractions
making all my actions
seem non-childlike
maybe not to others
but surely to me.

Look the other way

If I look the other way,
It doesn't mean that I didn't see,
doesn't mean that I don't know.
It doesn't mean that I am gullible
or naive
or stupid
or plain ole dumb.

What it does mean;
is that,
I looked the other way.

Man and Machine

In the empty night
a lonesome train
lets out a shrill wail
as if to complain.

You mortal men
Get off my lane
No time to stop
No time to explain.

Manic Depression – Wave 1
WASHED UP

There is a deep dark emptiness that I am in
I'm not sure how or when it all began.
The ebb and flow between hardship and ease,
leaves me stranded here lifeless,
like seaweed on the beach.

Manic Depression – Wave 2
BACK TO SEA

But soon the tide comes up to me
and gentle starts to wash my feet
and slowly lifts me up to sweep
me,
back to the waters, back to the deep.

Manic Depression – Wave 3
THE CURRENT

It is a lot like flying
there in the deep
drift into the stream of current and see
just where this cool current might lead,
me.
Hold out my arms and spread my wings
upon this current cool, I rise, I glide.
Partly here, partially hypnotized,
by the grandeur of the glorious deep,
the sensation that all is one with me.

MINDING HER OWN BUSINESS

She was minding her own business.
She was multi tasking
and she was good at it

driving down the road
putting lipstick on
singing to the radio
and texting on her cell phone
all while smoking a cigarette
and eating breakfast.

She didn't see that the traffic was stopped
and she never even hit her brakes.
She just slammed into that station wagon.
The investigators estimated her speed at around
60 to 70 miles an hour.

A baby in the station wagon lost it's life too.
It was in a car seat but it wasn't turned properly
and the air bag deployed and broke the poor baby's neck.

The baby's mother lived,
but she'll never live the same.
And all she was doing
was minding her own business.

MORNING DEW

Through the soft dry summer breeze
my heart and soul are ill at ease
for though we walked along the shore
our binding bond is there no more.

Quiet is the night still air
no breeze nor draft can find me there
for while I wait for the morning dew
my thoughts are all of me and you.

There we were, there was a time
when I was yours and you were mine.
But now that time has gone away
deep dark black and shades of grey.

Oh morning dew where do you lay?
For night time slipped on into day
and soon the hot sun shown through
with no trace nor feel of morning dew.

MY DESIRE

Don't want no shiny sunshine
don't want no shiny car
don't want no silly love song
don't want no cigarette
don't wanna smoke
don't wanna drink
don't want no one to want me
don't want no one to care
don't care about my socks, if they match or not;
I don't care if they are full of holes.
I don't care if I wear no underwear.
Don't care if my room's a mess.
Don't care if they shut the electricity off,
they can cut off my water too.

I don't want no dog.
Don't want no cat.
Not even a plant or a goldfish bowl;
I don't want nothing that might need me;
to feed it, or water it, or nurture it.

Not all of this is true.

MY MOJO

Her laughter is my mojo
her happiness my mirth
When my maiden is merry,
It's blossoms of cherry
I'm the Super-est man on earth.

Her sorrow is my kryptonite
her sadness is my curse,
When her love is cold,
all hell unfolds
I'm desert fields of dearth.

My objective

It is NOT my objective to be cute
nor is my objective to convince you
or win you
or flatter you
or anything to you.
It IS may objective to express myself
as clearly, as honestly,
as precise as I am capable.

For as three comes before four
score and seven years ago,
our fathers brought forth
then, hung their harps on the willow
and wept for Babylon. And with quills like chisels
carved on the snarling face of time these words:

Hello . . . . I love you . . . .
won't you tell me your name?

MY TEMPER

Tonight I lost my temper,
and for a minute I lost my soul.
I hate the things I said.
I hate I lost control.

I'll just have to do better.
But in retrospect I wonder,
what kind of man wouldn't have been upset?
No kind of man I know.

NIGHTSCAPES

Sometimes at night
I like to slip off,
steal away,
and listen.

I like to hear the sound on distant shore.
The ones far off that you can't ignore.
A barking dog, a fluttering sweet scented sheet,
the still small voice that beckons me,
crickets, traffic, acceleration and brakes:
It's all discreet; the sound of rubber on wet streets.

And sometimes rain's gentle fall,
it's all so easy to recall,
the distant sounds,
distinct and all.

I love the sound of far off things.
I love them all with a certain claim.
There is nothing to me that is quite as pure,
as the lovely sound of a distant train.

NOT RELIGIOUS, BUT

I don't know what it is
that makes me like that Old English.
I like a thou for a you
a shall for a will
I like willst thou for will you
I don't know why
Maybe it is the King James version
that I use to gobble up like a famished dog.
The Psalms just do not ring the same in the NIV
or the Amplified or even the "new" King James Version.
But in the old King James, the 1611 edition, it reads:

My heart panteth after Thee, Oh Lord!
As the hart panteth after the brook
so panteth my soul after thee.

Doesn't that read good?
The words roll off the tongue.
The vowels and consonants hold their own.
I like that Old English,
without apology.

NOVEL OLD NOVEL

It is too much like a novel
Just exactly like an Ayn Rand novel,
the government takes an inch
and then it floods right in.
Tsunamis of regulation
and bureaus
and reports.

(But this isn't a novel
this is real life 101.)

And the government becomes more and more
like that bohemeth bohemian from yonder lore
with rag-tag tentacles in every pore,
who turned into a woman
then became a whore,

glittering her way in with batting eyes
and lips of lies, moist sweet lies.
She'll reduce you to a beggar,
saying all things are common,
therefore all things to all.

Freedom should be defended with vigor,
against all tyrants
both foreign and domestic
at home or from abroad.
When good men do nothing
she advances some more.

NUMBERS

I ain't too good with numbers,
maybe I'm okay with the normal ones
but the tiny ones, they distract me.

I used to have dinner with a group of people,
it was a family of sorts.
We'd meet
and we'd eat
and when the check came,
rather than each one pitching in a ten or a twenty,
(or whatever was comfortable, or even nothing if need be
that would have been just fine with me
even a little better than fine
because as I said, I'm not real good with numbers,)
they would analyze to minutia.

The little numbers annoy me.
I'm not saying that that is the way that it should be.
I'm just saying that that is the way that it is.
Not many things annoy me as much as petty does.

They would always break out a calculator
(I'm not making this up)
and itemize what each one had
and then add the tax and matriculate the tip,
a delicate act since that ungrateful waitress
usually had the overwhelmingly annoying habit of
overlooking the ice in someones water.
They liked that waitress about as much as they liked me,
and it showed, oh yes, it showed.

By the way, I noticed that they were always
happy to figure the water into the tip. Zero!
Throw a zero into the mix and see what that does to your little
numbers.

But when they had finished this maticulous ritual
and lines were drawn in black and white
and there were columns and rows
and labels for names
this wasn't a game
this was about money,
each one would be directed as to how much they owed
for the meal and the tax and the tip. The comradery was free.
A woo hee hee.

I guess maybe it was a good thing that they did it that way.
Because I always knew exactly where I stood,
exactly where I stood,
right down to the last penny.

ONE HUNDRED FORTY FOUR YEARS AGO
(4-15-2009)

It was one hundred and forty-four years ago today.
a dozen dozen years - a *gross* of years.
That word spread like wildfire
across this land.

The President was DEAD!
He had been shot in the head,
and now he was dead.

Some foolish Southern Sympathizer
had imagined he was doing his people a favor
by killing The President of
The (soon to be re-) United States of America.

The President who had recently said:
"With malice toward none and charity toward all."
The President who thought it peculiar that men would own
other men like property.
The President who thought it peculiar that man would invoke
the assistance of
God in smothering his own brother.
The President who adroitly, almost single handedly,
kept The Union together.

I'm sure that some men rejoiced at the news of his death.
Me, I think what a terrible loss.
Even one hundred and forty-four years removed.

Paying Tithes

Whenever I eat at home
I'm faithful to pay my tithes to Max.
I always save at least a tenth for him.
He gets his at the end.
He knows that when he gets his, the meal is over
and he can quit looking at me
with those adoring eyes.

Peace

You tell me,
would it not
be good if
the whole world
slept in peace?
without hunger
or bloodshed
And the little
children didn't
believe their
teacher when
she tried to teach them
about an ancient custom
of man, **war**.
Would that not be good?

PIG-PEN

Some people need pens.
When I say pens, I'm talking pig.
Some people need pens
as pigs need a pig-pen.
Don't touch, don't feel, don't say.

For without a pen they would rush right out
and savor every morsel of life
and suck the bone dry
until nothing was left.
Then they would want to die,
not having anything to look forward to.

But with a pen they can pine,
and long to go beyond the realm,
and dream of the other side,
and fantasize;
about, stories that they had been told,
by other pigs, of the fold.

"Punked"

It hurts to realize that retardation
abides so deep inside my brain.

It's like I know I'm here and all
and I think I am thinking
but it is like I'm in an absurd, comic, tragic, play
all mixed into one big mess called "Me."
It is like I'm on candid camera
or I'm being "punked"
and someone is going to tell me any minute that this was just
a joke
just a hoax, and we will all laugh
and people will say that I was a good sport about it all,
that he dished it out, but he could take it too.
And maybe some will think that they would have cracked;
maybe some will think it would have been a piece of cake.

But they would be the ones who didn't see the pictures
the ones who didn't know the truth
who didn't see them frolic in the snow
who didn't see the videos
who didn't know what I know.

It not easy being inbreed
and being cognizant of the fact
that I use my brain
like a chimpanzee
uses a computer.

READING FACES

I think it might be good
if in our schools we taught our kids
the science of reading faces,
maybe it should be called an art,
I don't know . . . which ever is fine with me.

But it really isn't hard to learn
so it shouldn't be hard to teach
and it could be oh so beneficial.

Show a kid a photograph of a face
and ask him what he sees
It isn't being judgmental
in the usual sense of the word.
It is the use of the senses
which to me is what education is all about.

Look at a photograph
of someone who has abused their body
with improper drugs and alcohol
and maybe a touch of adultery here and there
and you can see it all laden in the lines,
in the shape of the smile, the squint of the eyes.

Look at a photograph
of a noble man . . . let's say . . . Lincoln.
You can see the firmness in his eyes.
(the resolution is there too.)
You can sense the sorrow from the past
The sorrows from Ann Rutledge all the way to Gettysburg
they are collected and compacted
right there upon his face.

Look at Sitting Bull.
You can read the lines
It wasn't the firewater that left those lines
It was hard living of another kind.

The opportunities are boundless
just go to the mall.
I've never met a soul without a face
and somehow or another
the two are embraced.

We should teach that to our kids.

THE COUPLE

Over at that table
the young man was trying to pay attention.
He was struggling to listen,
I could tell.

She was going on and on
about so and so, and such and such.
And he was trying, I know he was
but he really didn't give a flip.
He may have wanted to, but he didn't.

She knew it too but she had been cooped up in that house all
day
smoking cigarettes and thinking about
such and such, and so and so
and she was ready to vent.
They were not going to walk on her.

He had busted his ass all day.
His knuckles were busted too, and greased.
His jeans were gritty.
He didn't take the time to change his clothes because
she was hungry,
and in a hurry.

He wanted her to be happy.
They didn't stand a snowball's chance in hell.
I could tell.

kent

Was it me?

I don't know why the clouds all look so lonely.
I don't know why the trees they seem so sad.
I don't know why the birds they all quit singing.
Oh my, oh my, was it something that I said?

Star light, Star bright

I thought I had wished upon a star
She granted my wish that avatar
That we would have no distance between us
Lucky me!
For I had cast my wish upon the lap of Venus

SHORE GOT THE BLUES

Ain't got me no money
Ain't got me no car
Ain't got me no hopes
Of going to far
Ain't got me nobody
Ain't got me no you
But Lord have some mercy
I shore got da blues.

Don't much care about livin'
Don't care if I do
But I know that I know
I don't know what to do
Oh Lord have me some mercy
Cause I shore got them blues.
I could cry me a river
cause I shore got da blues.
Lord won't you have mercy?
Cause I shore got the blues.

Welcome to the USSA

Welcome to the United Socialist States of America
A tried and failed way of living.
Forget production,
just slosh money around.
More government is not the answer.
It is the problem!
Just look anywhere where there is federal money
and it is FUBAR. The reason is:
It deflates the value of a hard earned dollar.
A working man doesn't stand a sporting chance
when he is trying to compete with federal dollars.
His one dollar was worth about 27 federal dollars.
Because of this so called "stimulus bill"
tomorrow, or the day after, it will be worth 64 federal dollars.
The value of his dollar didn't go UP.
The value of the hard earned dollar compared to a federal
dollar went down
because there are so many more of them to compete against.
Our forefathers from the South would not have signed that
Constitution without the tenth amendment being attached.
This is encroachment!
Welcome to: The USSA.

SOMETIMES

Sometimes love comes
like cool rain
to a parched dessert

and flowers of thankfulness bloom
as far as the eye can see.

SOS—SAME OLD SONG

surely they are right
surely I'm just nascent and simple
and I really hadn't thought it out
surely man is destined to stay on this path
this path to war . . . this damned path to war.

They are always stirring it up.
Always some big threat on the horizon
After a while you can predict
Watch them make a boogey man out of China.

And we'll stumble over some stumbling-stone such as Taiwan,
and here we go again. Hundreds of thousands are dead.
Because we've got such good weapons now.
Isn't it ironic that with each new (read old) war
the weapons of the winner are always "state of the art".
"Look how this here cannon will kill another man.
Hell, it will blow him to smithereens."

From a rock
to a stick, to a spear with flint for a tip
to a bow and arrow, to a knife, to a sword
To a rifle, you can see where I'm going here.
I'm going all the way up or down to splitting an atom.

"Hey looky here, this here bomb can kill millions in seconds
and when it's done won't nothing grow for
thousands of years. Even if it grew, couldn't nothing eat it. This
here weapon is state of the art. Let's start a war and see how it
works.".

and they cry Peace Peace
When there is no Peace
and they stir up shit
and throw salt in their eyes
and then they ask, What's the matter?
Are you not a peaceful man?

It's the same old song
twenty-ninth verse.

STORM CLOUDS ON THE HORIZON

Storm clouds on the horizon
there's thunder over there
it will soon be raining hard again
storm winds are gonna blow

You called again tonight
said you was going to be working late
I know you know I got caller id
and the caller id said you was calling from "My Friends Place"

Strom clouds are coming my way
it always seems to go that way
when you don't even try to hide your ways
do it right out in the open.

Big bad storm is coming my way
The wind and rain will blow
we'll do that two-steps and your gone again
cold dark empty in my soul.

Swinger of Trees

I too have been a swinger of trees.
But not of the birch variety.
Sweetgum!
We swung sweetgum trees.
Finding one that wasn't too tall,
for it would surely break
before it would take
you back to earth.
Finding one that wasn't too small
lest you couldn't crawl
to the top, before it plopped
you right back to where you'd been.
But scouting for one just right
and high enough
and limber enough
and stiff enough
and branches just right
you could ride such a tree
from heaven to earth
and gently land on land
and do it again and again.

THAT SLIPPERY HEART

The heart, it is another thing.
You really can't wrestle with it
because you can never pin it down
you can never get your arms around it
you can never get a grip
just when you think . . . there you go thinking again . . .
but just when you think
you have it figured out
it goes slipping
and morphing into some . . . .
god knows what . . . into some . . . . thing else.
Like a greased pig it slips away
and gets away, and goes running off.
How can one love with that?
You can't. You just stand in your corner
try to figure it . . . there you go thinking again.
You can't think the heart.
It don't think. It just slips and slides
and runs away.
Leaving you to think . . . .
What the Fuck?

The awakening

Wakened without cause one night
no sound nor shake me stirred
but very much to my surprise
I awakened to find me dead.

There was nothing then for me to do
nothing for me to see
and much as I had suspected
there was nothing for me to be.

So I shrugged my shoulders to slumber
and with a folding of my hands
while nothing there, surrounded me there
I drifted on back to sleep.

THE AZTEC

Txatchanmuxiatia had been chosen!
It was bestowed upon him
the high honor of connections
to the gods.
He would thank them,
appease them,
bless them,
calm them,
even make them cry.

He had dreamed of such a day,
he and a million other men.
But this year at the apex of the Sun
He would be the One, life was complete.

He always knew his daughter was special.
He told her the good news first, even before he told his mate.
She beamed that big beaming smile for which she was known.
They hugged each other and cried tears of joy,
and tears of sorrow.

At the appointed time they walked to the mountain top together.
Thousands and thousands of people watching.
They stood there. Together. Waiting.
Waiting for the horn to blow, signaling the apex exact.
Just as the horn was about to blow he began, lifting her up,
kissing her cheek on the way up, their eyes meet, she was smiling.
He lifted her high above his head, the horn blew . . . .
He threw her off the mountain.

Txatchanmuxiatia stood arched,
his proud face stretched toward the heavens,
his breast arched toward the gods,
tears streamed down his cheeks
arms held wide open, fingers extended.
He was taking it in . . .
He was One with everything.
The wind blew his hair.
And the Sun started his descent.

The Carnivore

Some girls
most girls
look for boys to kiss.

But she
she
looks for men to devour.

The Compliment

She was very complimentary.
She said that she was nervous
to meet new people.

I was flattered,
but I had to confess,
I'm not new: I'm forty-seven.

THE DAY I DIED

The day I died
was just like any other day
the wind was hot
the world was mean
but it was just like any other day
the day I died
excepting one small
almost imperceptible thing.
the day I died
she was there
and though it was so ephemeral
and so fleeting
so swift to the naked eye
that no one would have noticed
but she was there
and her soft hand
felt my forehead and my brow
and I could feel her hot tears
as they feel down upon my cheek
and her salty tears tasted
like cool fresh rain.
Other than that
it was all the same.
The same hot wind
the same cold world
not even bidding godspeed.

The Divorce

in an itty-bitty room
in an itty-bitty court
in an itty-bitty town
in an itty-bitty state,

there was a big broad bench,
a large leather chair,
a huge head rest,
comfort galore: comfort to spare.
and on this throne there smugly sat

an itty-bitty Judge
and his itty-bitty hand
took an itty-bitty gavel.

I looked him in his itty-bitty eyes
read his itty-bitty mind
and my itty-bitty ears
heard an itty-bitty tap
as his itty-bitty mouth,
gave her
      an itty-bitty
           everything.

The early worm

If the early bird
gets the worm,
then the early worm
is better off asleep.
goodnight!

THE ELEPHANT

There was an elephant
there in the room with us.
Nobody mentioned it.
We sat and talked about
all kinds of stuff
but nobody mentioned
the elephant,
nor the elephant shit
that stunk up the room.

We did discuss the weather
and the past
and the present
and the niceties
and the gray hair
but not the elephant
there in the room
with all of us.

There was an elephant there
in the room with us.
Hell, why not mention it?
We all knew it was there.
So big and cumbersome
with hide as tough as elephant hide,
but it didn't hide, it stuck out
like a sore elephant
there in the room with us.
Next time, I'm going to talk
about that balnkety-blank elephant
there in the room with us.

The Flood

They say it is a depression
better yet, just a dang'd recession
my head then goes a guessin'
with all these wheels a messin'
with their trillion dollar schemes
it sometimes seems obscene
it may trickle down or up
everything has run amuck
but it seems to me
with a million million bucks
There's bound to be a flood.
Somewhere.

THE LIVING PART

It's not the dying part that is hard for me.
It's the living part that's not so easy.
Trying to find my keys
paying bills all prompt and clean
the dirty laundry
the empty cans
the unmade bed
the un-maiden bed
the thank-you notes
the birthdays
anniversaries
the funerals; and all the stuff of life
that fills the in between.

It's a struggle for me to live
like a normal person should;
clean socks and a clean truck,
credit cards in order,
the fresh scent of flowers,
the feel of normal sleep.

I'll get this living thing down before long
and they'll call me Mr. Clean,
and I'll cherish this life and living
and the short span of life
that lingers like vapor
from birth to death
and all the mess
that dogs me in between.

THE MOUSE

The little mouse
runs so fast against the floor.
It must think that I don't love it
love him or her, any more.

Because it runs so fast, so hard
running across the floor.
It rams its head against the base
of my chair.

I look down at him, or her
as they give their head a shake,
it ask me; "what was all of that for?"

I don't know I said,
It was your mistake,
as he or she, scampered through the door.

THE OAK TREE

It was an old oak tree
we both agreed
but we varied by degrees
on just how old this tree might be.
he was guessing a hundred
I said: seventy-five
neither one of us knew.
But there was an old barbed wire
buried deep within the tree
grooves that had grown around
that bore witness to another time.
When some farmer had tried to hem in
some cattle
or pear trees
or something that was his.
That he didn't want to wander off
or somehow be left for loss
or be mistaken for some other's handiwork.
But that was another time long ago
when someone didn't want to let go
of something that he thought was his
but we had a job to do, today.
One hundred he said.
My guess was half plus one half, seventy-five.
We were careful not to hit the blade.
One hundred-twenty-five dollars we saved that way.
But he was more right than I.

It was *over* one hundred years ago.
We counted the rings.
It was over one hundred years ago
that some farmer ate his breakfast
and probably kissed his wife.
Said he was going to fence in the back forty,
protect what was theirs,
perhaps prevent some strife.

THE ONLY THING IN COMMON

The only thing they had in common,
was the fact that they were both born
members of the opposite sex.
And children, they had that in common too.

THE PRESIDENTS

Night pervading through the trees
saplings at heart
but standing strong
against the dark-dark wind.

Only to fall headlong
and lie in state
while critters crawl and feast

until all is gone
but a pound of dirt,
and whispers of the leaves.

THE REPLY

There is an answer there
It's laced in the blank display
The glaring lack of words
The things you didn't say

THE RIDE

I did not drive
for I was driven to drink
so a sober one drove.
again

THE RIVER

The river floods at eighteen feet.
Today it crest at forty-one feet.
How am I suppose to sleep,
-with water lapping at my sheet?

THE SHORTEST POEM

I

The Trade

What would you take
for the next couple of years of your life?
What price would you command?
What price *could* you command?
What would you take in exchange
for the next couple of years of your life?
Fifty thousand? Two million? Priceless?

another year on the couch
another drink
another cigarette
a book, a movie, a game
a dame
a headache.

Probably you will take
about what you took.
It is right there on line 28
on the form 1040.
That plus a few incidentals
is what you traded your life for,
just last year.

The truth is:
That is what you traded your life for,
and the odds are that you will do it
again and again
until you die.

THE TRIP

He tripped upon a twig
a teeny tiny twig.
Catching his balance
he looked back
and said: "What the hell that did me trip?"
looking down he saw
It was nothing but a twig
a teeny tiny twig.

THIS VIEW

I want to hold you, sometimes.
And feel you breath beneath my wing.
And tell you to hold on,
we might reach new heights.

I want to hold you, most times,
let you warm breath
fill my mind,
and tell you that this view,
is all I've ever known.

THESE TWO

Oh, I understand a lot of things,
I know how a shoestring
is suppose to work
though sometimes only in theory.
I get the gist of geometry.
I know what a one-eighty is.
I can identify a triangle.
It has three sides I'm sure.
But acute and obtuse are bit obscure.

I know a little about a lot of things.
Even less do I know about me,
but I'm learning a little each day.
I know I don't put much value in things.
Things are all too tangible.
I know I value relationships,
and will go out of my way to mend fences,
though I don't know what fences are for.

I know I will die and I think of that a lot
not with fear or dread or distain.
But I will put it off as long as I can,
I'm in no way eager to go.
I've seen enough of this world,
the Grand Canyon and Niagara Falls too.

I've heard enough,
felt enough,
tasted enough.
I've done enough,
saving only love
and oxygen.

I know that I need
these two.

DEEP ROOTED SHADE TREE

Julia,
You need to know
that I am one happy little boy.
I love even just the sound of your name.
Julia.
It just kind of rolls off the tongue. Julia-
Oh, and I like Juliette too.
It kind of rolls off the tongue and then stops.
Juliette.

Happy,
Happy,
Happy,
Happy,
I like the way 'Happy' sounds too.
Oh my! I even like that sentence.
Say it yourself and listen to it.
I like the way 'Happy' sounds too.
Oh my,
I am one happy little boy I am, Julia.
And it is all because of you.

kent

Too many

Never hoed a row that didn't need hoein'
Never knew no girl that didn't need knowin'
Never read no verse that didn't need readin'
Never shot wild game that didn't need eatin'
Never ate no orange that didn't need peelin'
Never killed no man that didn't need killin'

But I know that I've thought
too many a thoughts
that didn't need thinkin'

TOO SIMILAR

It is nothing more than just another religion
At least is *seems* like nothing more
Than just another religion.
Nobody really believes
But they can quote the creeds
From left to right
And upside down
And all the in betweens.

It is just another dogma
Some *kind* of warmed over dogma.
Where they speak of Freedom
And Liberty
And Equality
While they shekel and chain their brother
And build fences to rebuke their neighbor
And make war to spread there their faith

It reminds me of The Church so much
I'm starting to have a hunch
They are both in cahoots
It gives me the poots
The Government
And
The Church.

Was it wrong

Was it wrong for us to dare to trod
where angels dream to fly?
To spill our love on a moonlit beach
before the rising tide?

And was it wrong for us to tip the cup
and laugh before we cry?
To taste a sip of wanton love
and live before we die?

Was it wrong for us to feel the touch
that yearns from down inside?
To intertwine our hearts and minds
our bodies, you and I.

Soaring, sailing, softly now
the rhythm of the tide.
As crashing waves
from all around
send salt-spray to the sky.

Pleasant, pure, and poignant still
the memories we derived.
I doubt not now,
between right or wrong.
No love can be a lie.

WE TOO SHALL PASS

We must all go to the grave.
Some go kicking and screaming.
Others dig in their heels and are dragged.
Some do a swan dive
and give a good stiff middle finger
to the rest of the world as they succumb.
Some leap in head first
and don't even make a ripple
and I want to hold up a sign that says give them a ten.
Others go unnoticed
and no one even sees.
But we all must go,
eventually.

What do you do?

If someone you'd like
to see satisfied
would only be satisfied
if you were
cut up into little pieces
castrated in the public square
eyes burnt out with flaming rods
flesh boiled in boiling vats
the body properly identified
so that everyone knew
it belonged to you.

If someone like that
you want to satisfy
but you don't want to die
Tell me then,
Tell me,
What is it that you do?

WHAT FUN!

Wow, what a great idea!
I just saw on my myspace page
where I could date married women
right here, in my area!

WOW!
How exciting!

Bring me a big bowl of drama,
and a side dish of adultery.
I'll just drink water with lemon.
For dessert, I'll have . . . .
Well, I'm really not sure.

WHAT THE?

I know some girls who eat real well
and then sneak to the bathroom
and run their finger down their throat
and purge, they call this anorexic.

I know other girls who pay to tan
they tan all over, I mean naked.
But when it comes time for them to show me
where their tan lines aren't
they become all tanorexic.

WHEN YOU LEAVE

Go a head and leave me
you know I'm not one to beg
but just do me one favor
before you leave, I ask just one favor of you.
Would you take my heart with you
would you take it when you go
I don't want it hanging around here messing up my head.
Don't want it hanging around, bringing me down,
acting a clown and messing with my head.
So if you're gonna leave me
Go ahead and leave me, but won't you do me just one favor
take my heart with you, take it when you go.
I'm tired of it leading me around, acting a clown
I don't want it anymore.
It is kind of broken anyway,
but you might could use it for a doorstop.
Or a paper weight, or you can throw it in the river for all I
care.
I just know that I don't want it, don't want it anymore
It's not my friend.
Please take my heart with you,
- take it when you go.

WHO THE HELL DO YOU THINK YOU ARE?

Who the hell do you think you are? he ask.
I always want to chuckle when I hear that question.
I try to hold the chuckle back, (I'm always trying not to laugh)
lest he think I'm not serious enough
well hell, he has enough seriousness for three or four
what would he do with a little more
from me?
only get more serious I guess,
hard to imagine.

He says: "I said, who the hell do you think you are!?"
a few more decibels louder this time.
Oh no, I think, this is really sounding serious now.
It is an age old question, but I ponder it some more.

I ask him, "Who the hell do I think I am?"
Yes, he says: "Who the hell do you think you are?"
I'm inclined to give him a tap, his record is stuck,
but I'm quite sure he would perceive I struck,
and challenged his manhood.
we hold different views on manhood too, I'm pretty sure.

Let me see, Who do I think I am?
I'm tempted to tell him that
it is none of his business who I think I am,
and it is none of my business what he thinks of me.
But I don't think that will fly.

Let me see:
I look like me
I feel like me.
I smell like me.
I'd bet good money that I taste like me
but I always have
and all things are relative, so I can't be sure
for I have nothing to compare me to.
Being me is all I have ever known.

He interrupts, "Who in the fuckin' hell do you think you are?"
I know, I know, I'm thinking here
you can see I'm a little slow.
Who do I THINK I am?
I'm going to say . . . .
I think I am ME . . . . final answer.

WHY . . . ?

I wasn't ashamed
to ask God why,
The Good on Earth
are so quick to die.

Quick, not curt, was His reply:
My son on Earth
what could I do?
We need angels here
in heaven too.

The Blackberried Lawyer

Sometimes I have to re-remind myself that lawyers have souls too.
Sometimes I catch myself thinking bad thoughts.
Sometimes these thoughts morph into questions.
Sometimes good questions, sometimes bad questions,
Sometimes funny questions, but always real questions.
Questions like this: Do you know why it is a good thing that lawyers have souls?
Because God needs something else to burn when their bodies are gone.

Anytime I have business around or near the courthouse I'm always reminde of "a den of Thieves". Often our attempts at Justice are little more than absurd, comic, farce masquerading as Justice.

I was having a hard time trying to decide which one I needed to be more concerned about; Him or Her. She had been abused all of her life; mentally, physically, sexually. And she was beginning to show the symptoms of acute diabetes. He, on the other hand, was a lawyer. He had his bulging piles of paperwork and his sharp pressed suit, a good haircut and his Blackberry too. He was picking up money at such a fast pace that he couldn't even see the tender soul that was in front of him. She had hired him to represent her. She needed to get her Disability and she needed Medicaid more than she had ever needed anything in her whole life. But he needed to make his next appointment. He had forgotten that helping others was the only reason that The Law had attracted him in the first place.

She was a child in need, but *he* was too far gone.
She deserved to be helped, but *he* deserved to be pitied.

He had determined that I had nothing of importance to impart even though his client had been living in my home for nine months. He didn't need me as a witness. He had also declined the opportunity to have State Certified witnesses who were willing and eager to testify on her behalf. He had sweep me, and them, aside like so much of the other human debris that gets in his way. To him, anything that slows his pace is just debris and is swept aside. He was too busy to grant me even thirty minutes of his precious time.

His Excellency was busy.

He was even too busy to find the time to read the letter which I had taken a great deal of effort to comprise and then to condense. I had comprised the letter because I care about her. I had condensed the letter because I was concerned about The Judge's time. I knew that The Judge was busy. I wanted every sentence to count. But it didn't matter that I had specific and material information concerning his client's petition, concerning his client's condition. The lawyer didn't find the time to give The Judge his copy of the letter either. He told me, after the hearing, that he would submit the letter, later. He said that the letter would become a part of her case file, later.

It appeared to me that the letter was irrelevant to him because it would only slow him down and he likes to run fast. He knew all about efficiencies and maximizations. He knew how to quantify and he knew about the magic of compound interest. It was in his best interest that his client not be heard now. Oh she would be heard, not now, but later. He looked at the clock. He had to run. So he deftly, adroitly, single handedly, and without fanfare managed to get her case deferred for a few more months, practically guaranteeing for himself the same sized piece of an even bigger pie. All the while guaranteeing with certainty her continued demise, which as I said, to him, was irrelevant. She didn't matter: Just look at *Her*. She wasn't his *client*. She was just another meal ticket for one fine dinner that he would savor, later. She weeps at the world. She is nauseous and her feet are numb and her fingers tingle. Her toenails are peeling off.

I scramble to get her the "correct" insulin that she needs. The kind that they don't pass out at the Open Hands Clinic. The *Humalin 70/30*. The kind that cost 60 dollars for a quarter of an ounce. The kind that when I pay for , I can't help but think about how incredibly hot that hell is going to be. I can't help but wonder if it is wrong for me to be glad about that.

PART II

Dedicated to Julia
Who taught me to see the world
In Fun Colors

ZOMBIES

That is what they are.
They are Zombies.
Walking around in public.
Driving their cars in public places.
At the intersection.
At the grocery store.
Out in public places.
Dead people walking . . .
Dead people talking . . .
on expensive cell phones
That is what they are.
Zombies
That is what they are.
They are Zombies.
Walking around in public.
Driving their cars in public places.
At the intersection.
At the grocery store.
Out in public places.
Dead people walking . . .
Dead people talking . . .
on new fangled cell phones
They are Zombies.
Walking around in public.
Driving their cars in public places.
At the intersection.
At the grocery store.
Out in public places.
Dead people walking . . .
Dead people talking . . .
on so-called smart cell phones

WORKS

If a brother or sister is naked
and destitute of daily food
and you say unto them: depart in peace
be ye warmed and filled.
Notwithstanding you give them not
that which is needful for the

body
What doth
it profit?
For as the body
without the spirit is
dead
even so faith without
works
is dead.
Show me thy faith without thy
works
and I will show thee my faith by my works
Was not Abraham our Father justified by works
when he offered Isaac his son upon the alter?
Seeth thou how faith wrought with his works
and by
works
was faith made perfect.

James—the brother of Jesus—to the twelve tribes, scattered
abroad.

WOMEN

I can't imagine why God
made women so.
I wonder on earth
if even He knows.

But I'm seeing a pattern
in His handy work scheme.
Seventy-five thorns
for one single rose.

WHY NOT . . . ?"

Why run?
I ask myself.
Why do you run?
Who wouldn't run I say?
Didn't you hear her say:
I love you.

Where Did It Go?

I had the perfect poem
inside my head,
it was just a minute ago.

I swore I would remember
but you know how these things go.

It was a poem about a newfound love
about life being complete.

But I swear for the life of me,
I wonder, where did that good poem go?

WHEN PIGS FLY

I wonder if the clause-
when pigs fly-
has anything to do
with swine flu.

WHAT IS

dark shrouds
eternity
never the mind
of what will be
what is
is
what will be
will be
always tomorrow
dark
eternity.

Villanova.

I liked watching Villanova.
They had a philosophy that I liked
Survive and advance.
Isn't that good?
Do your best to advance but first
you survive.
Survive the whirlwind
Of adolescence and youth
Survive the struggle
the search for the truth.
Raise your own children
the best that you can
marry them off and survive.
Survive till you are planted
and plant till you die.

VEGAS

I worry about you
there in Vegas.

The night crowd scuffles around like zombies.
The lights burn all the time.
Three a.m. looks like three p.m.
from inside.
Always burning
burning never ends
like the lights that flash perpetually
screaming for attention
in a town . . . in a city . . . in a town
of attention whores.

The smell of hopes vanished
Boulevard of Broken Dreams
The Strip is stripped, of life
true life,
vibrant life.

And now they go through the motions
imitating life.
The smell of bourbon, vodka, and beer
lingers in the air.

It's Vegas

I worry about you there.

UPSIDE DOWN

Night and day
Dark and light
Black and white
shades of gray.

Soft and hard
earth and sky
dusk and dawn
She and I.

UNTIL THEN

Truth can be independently verified
by any disinterested third party.
Until then, it is merely speculation.
*

TWILIGHT TRIMIGHT

Now I lay me down to sleep
and wonder about my baby sweet
wonder what she is thinking now
I wander off and wonder how, or if
that cow really jumped over the moon
It seems fairy tale-ish I know
but if a beanstalk can grow that tall
and humpty dumpy fell off the wall
who am I to say?:
"Cows can't jump over the moon that way."
If I were a cow, I think I'd try to too.

TRAIN OF TOMORROW

When I was younger
I could see tomorrow on the horizon
Coming toward me
Like a fast moving train
Steady and constant
always approaching
I tried to scoop up bits of stuff
That I could caste upon her
When tomorrow became today.
In an instant, or maybe two at most
Tomorrow became today
and just as quickly
slipped on into yesterday
What the hey? I'd say
I didn't have time for the stuff
Slow down at the portal
You know I'm a mortal
Why must you speed so much?
Looking back at tomorrow receding
I regretted there was no repeating
Until I heard a faint sound
and turned back around
It was easy to see
there coming at me
tomorrow was coming back
to give me another crack.
Hooray! Hooray! and yeah!

TORN

Part of me is gearing up
getting ready to do it again
ready to turn the page
and start another chapter.

Another part of me is tired
and is growing lethargic
willing to just take a rest
and coast through life for a while.

I am a true Gemini
split in two from head to soul
part of me is steady and strong
the other part, a growing part
doesn't seem to know.

Too damn happy

I saw her again tonight.
We crossed paths
in the isle at the store.
She had an overwhelming smile.
I couldn't help but wonder
what was wrong this time?
Had there been a death
of someone close?
Had she just witnessed a bad wreck
where someone lost their head?
Her smile was much too radiant
and there was a certain sparkle in her step.
I know her well enough to know
that she isn't happy
unless someone is hurting.
The harder the hurt the bigger the smile.
I couldn't quite put it together
And as I drove from the store
I perused the landscape
looking for police cars and ambulances
conglomerated together.
Everything was normal.
Nothing stood out.
All I knew, and I knew it for certain
was that somewhere, someone
was in a heap of pain
in a world of hurt.
I was sorry that it was them
but more glad it wasn't me,
No, not this time.

TO ERR IS HUMAN

to err is human,
to moo bovine.

THOUGHT ON THOUGHT

Thought might not be quantifiable
which means you can't judge it physically
i.e. you can't weigh it in grams
measure it in inches
read temperature in degrees of Kelvin.

Thought is . . . in my opinion . . . qualify-able.
which means you can measure its
aesthetic properties or attributes.
i.e. you can weigh it and evaluate
the thought into relation to what you
judge to be good or bad.

I believe I know (an interesting phrase) good from bad.

where does the thought fit in?
Is it true?
Would it bear good fruit?
Will it benefit everybody involved?
Is it legal?
—legality really only establishes
— lines of minimally accepted behavior.
Would I want my children to be as I am thinking?

THIS WORLD

This world is not my home.
I'm just a passing through.
Until a better world comes along,
this one will have to do.

THIS MESS THAT YOU MADE

Just trying to carry on
just trying to make sense
of the mess that you made.

Just trying to live normal
and act all sane and all
Just trying to make sense of it all
the mess that you made.

Lonely days blend
into lonely nights.
The nights grow larger and darker
the mess that you made.

picking up the pieces
trying to make them fit
one big jigsaw puzzle
without a pattern
or even sides
what a mess that you made!

I can't say that I don't care
although I try and I try
I *can* say that I don't want you
sure don't want to hold you
look at me now
this mess that you made.

The Two Margarets

The saddest lines that I have ever read
were on the face of Margaret Hatcher's head.
They spoke of sorrow,
they spoke of pain.
They told the story
of a woman betrayed.
And I never knew the cause, the root.
I wondered if the point was moot.
If the pain was real,
or self conceived.
The hurt would hurt about the same,
whether from false belief, or certain blame.
But the lines were so sad;
They hollered loud of a wounded heart,
not a broken leg, which could be reset,
and made like new again.
But a heart when broken, shattered like that
is never made quite right again.
The gladdest lines I have ever read
Were on the face of Margaret Johnson's head.
They told the story of a ripened age
a life that was full of trials, trips and falls.
Her heart was courageous, fit, and intact.
I know the lines were all in their heads.
But if given a choice,
I would choose the latter,
and save the sad for sport.

THE TALL HOG

He had to be the tall hog
at the trough.
He'd push the others around
and was proud of the fact
that he said what he thought.

He'd piss where he wanted
and shit where he would.
If others didn't like it,
it was all the more good.

He could sit and philosophize
with the best of them
but there in the pen
he made life ugly
for all of his kin.

The Not You

I know that the you I knew
is nothing more than a pigment of my imagination.
I know that you are not the you that I thought I knew
for you are neither kind
nor polite, nor sweet
nor loving, nor caring.
But for so long
I believed a lie.
You said: "I love You."
But you lied.
Time and Time again.

When you were out
on the town
chasing god knows who
you were not being good
like you said.
You lied, you lied.
Time and Time again.
Oh, I guess I knew it then.
But I didn't want to see.
I didn't want The Third Degree.

Cognitive Dissonance
I think it is called.
It is quite common
when people don't see
what is so plain for all to see.
So I guess my love was not for you.
It was for the you that I thought I knew.
It was for the NOT you.

THE NEXT TIME

The next time I solicit a roommate
I think I should give them fair warning.
Warning: Living with this person
may be harmful to your mental, physical, and spiritual well
being.

Sometimes I just shake my head at me.
Look at you boy.
What's up with this room?
Are you a baboon?
Put dirty clothes here
Clean clothes there.
Is that chocolate syrup there
spilled all over the nightstand?
Was that deliberate?
Doesn't that stuff attract ants?
Are you trying to be attractive,
or does that just come natural?

I could go on and on about the weaknesses of me.
Many times if given a choice
I wouldn't want to live with me either
but I don't know how to
get away from me
and I don't do good
at trying to get housebroken,

maybe a simple disclaimer
would cover all bases.

The Mosaic

This day is but another piece
that I will place
by choice
or by default.

Shards of glass are each day
Way does lead on to way
each piece refracts
prisons are full, painted gray.

Murals big and grand
small pieces merged to One.
Stand back to see the big picture
light scattered against night.

The glory or the shame
I am man
I shape, I make
either by default
or by design.

The choice is made either way
The picture there is mine to paint
My fervent hope and silent prayer
is that this piece of glass
would look good there.

THE HEART.

It's the heart.
If it wasn't for that heart,
man, I'd have it made.
But my heart can hardly stand
on his own two feet,
like a man.
He just lays there beaten up,
— goofy, skinless, and fragile.
If it wasn't for that heart,
man, I'd have it made.
Like a big ole pig in a waller,
just laying in the sun.

The Hardest Part

The hardest part
is parting with her.
We've been through so much
together
and not together at times
when she carried the weight of The Shoppe
on her back, as I meandered aimlessly,
when my vision was bad
and my speech was slurred
self-sedated in vain futile attempts
to find comfort or meaning
in a second divorce . . . and the kids.

Other times when we took on dozens all at once
just the two of us, never flinching or backing up
in fact, leaning forward, in full advance.
"How may I be of service?" she always ask.
and by gosh she is . . . . Always of service.
She is a busy bee of Public Service.

I'm going to be like her someday
when I grow up.

The hardest part is parting with her, Charity
even if that parting
is just a little ways down the street.

THE FULL MOON.

The moon is always full.
It doesn't always look that way.
It is because of our perspective,
that it doesn't always seem that way.

The light always hits the moon full-faced,
just like it does on earth.
But from where I sit it always changes.
It is the bestest clock for earth.

THE FLAME

It only last for a spark.
One sharp smart spark
of burst into a flame.
It is only for one soft spark.
Wild moths determined to flutter
their last full sputter
headlong into the attractive
consuming flame.

THE DOLLAR GENERAL

people walking around
like zombies
hand to ear
stuck on cell phones.
brains oblivious
to the sounds
of life around them
the sounds of children
reaching up
and sounds of children's laughter
children crying
horns in the distant
grocery carts clanging
people speaking
in monotone.
feet shuffling
mouths murmuring
cashier explaining
patrons complaining
zombies lifeless
on cell phones.

Me, in the way.
@ Dollar General

The City

Out there in the hinder lands
out there along the ridge
out there in the countryside
there is a road
and it is wide enough
and it long enough
and it is tough enough
and smooth enough
But it doesn't bring them in
like the roads in the city do.
The roads in the city are streets
and the streets run North and South
and East and West
And the people come from far and wide
to the City.
One may meet a Jamaican
a Brazilian
a Japaneseian
or even a Chineseian
I've meet no one from farther than China.
Sometimes we talk with our hands
I've learned to say good like Yum-Yum
I ask if they would like a drink
by holding my hand toward my mouth
and tipping it up as if I have a cup, in my hand.
I know one universal sign besides the dollar.
It is a smile.
And laughter sounds good in any language.
And laughter comes easy when feelings are good.
I belong in the city.
The feuds are all over my head.
And I can mingle
with my pockets a jingle
. . . . . . and laughter on my lips.

THE BEAST

Sometimes at night
loneliness slips up on me
like leprosy
and my problems loom large
like a famished beast
that soon will devour me.
I can feel her mocking me
behind my back.
I know it is just an illusion
some sort of a delusion
for I know that no problem
is really that big
that people of all walks
of all ages have worried
about problems that didn't
amount to a hill of beans.

I worry about my mind sometimes
I'm afraid confusion is settling in
I can stave her off for a little while
but that beast is gonna get me,
gonna eat me up and I can't even
lift my mind to resist.

The abyss

Someday, I'm afraid
the abyss is going to be
too deep, and
too dark, and
too impossible
to pull myself out of.

Someday, I'm afraid
may be here today.
Because it sure is deep
and it sure is dark
and I'm not even sure
if I want to try
any damn more.

SWEET SLEEP

If I had some sleeping pills just now,
the good kind,
I'm inclined to think
I'd take them all,
and give a damn
if I ever woke again.

SUNLIGHT

The best disinfectant is sunlight
just try for yourself and see
and the roaches flee
as does the mildew and mold
the rats and the mice
yes, even the lies;
(I only know a little of lice).
watch the rotten and the rotters,
scramble for darkness.
They
scamper for night.

SUICIDE SLOWLY.

She was large
she was fat
she didn't care
that her wig didn't match.

She was killing herself slowly
with sugar, salt, and fat.
She'd parked out front
reserved for the handicapped.

She'd decided to go
a long time ago.
She'd decided to go slowly
No one would ever know.

So she bought cupcakes and candy
and sweetness galore
Chocolates and sugar,
love like a whore.

When someone balked,
she just smiled.
Her ticket was punched.
If they didn't understand,
it was because, she was drunk.

Stretch

You cannot satisfy insatiable.
You cannot do just right the first time,
that which has become undone.
All you can do:
Is tell a few jokes
Try to have some fun
See if you can touch the moon
While reaching for the Son.

STORM

I really enjoy a good storm
especially at night.
I like to go outside and listen.
You can hear the center of attention
just beyond the ridge.

Deep thunder rolls across the land.
Sometimes it sounds like war
which always makes me sad.
When I think of some little boy
crouched with his ever present, god like sister
beneath the bed as shells reign down from heaven.

His little life will never be the same,
would to god that instead of bullets, he'd heard rain.
Like I did.

Some June Night

Just two bodies groping
two bodies groping together
in the dark
with the moon light
and the fire flies
and dogs in the background
barking
at some full moon
and the sweet feel
of soft breast
and moist breath
and I love you's in the dark.

SMOKIN'

The rain is fallin'
the frogs are croakin'
The crickets are crickin'
and me, I'm smokin'
some primo chicken.

SHE

There is a big hole there,
where She is suppose to be.
A great big gapping hole,
and no one even knows, but me.
and you, now.

(*She* is Emma Joelle)

SHE AND I

She was my Julia Roberts
my Ann Archer
my Demi Moore
all rolled into one.

She was my Gwyneth Paltrow
my Cristina Appelgate
my lovely Mary
from There's Something about Mary
But mostly she was Laura Dern
LuLa from Wild at Heart.

I was her Goober
and Gomer from Mayberry.
I was her darling Barney Fife too.
but more and more I was Wilson from Castaway
And oh, I was also her Gilligan
—for he was a castaway too.

SEVEN YEAR DREAM

(9-11-2008)

Seven years ago,
It still seems like a dream,

Planes still full
of people and fuel;
children with mommies,
fathers and pilots,
attendants and miscreants like me.

Crashing into buildings
deliberate death of man.
Buildings made by man, for man,
reaching up to heaven
toward heaven, relentless ascent of man.

Gathered from every nation-
each brotherhood and tongue-
brothers come back together-
Back from,
Back to . . . . what is it?
Is it . . . . Babylon?

The Lucky Number Seven.
It still seems such a dream.
Airplanes into buildings.
Buildings into the ground.
People killing people,
Man on top of man.

Vulgar: Obscene.
Awaken me! Awaken me!
From this . . . . Is this?
just an American Dream?

S/HE AND HE.

Yes it was a very true story. Any business around, near, or in the courthouses reminds me of a den of thieves. Hey, there's a poem in there somewhere.

This poor soul was one of several poor souls that my conscience wouldn't let me ignore. She was a sad, sad case. First of all she was a female who was some how or another trapped within a male body. While I can only guess about her anatomy, I know that s/he had to constantly struggle to suppress a persistent growth of facial hair. Her hands were perfectly suited for basketball. Her personality and thought processes were exactly identical to many females which I have known. She was particularly cautious to wear a bra at all times but it appeared to support nothing more than an average man's breast. She had the misfortune of being brought into this world from a mother who had conceived her in a relationship with a man who was not her spouse. Her mother was married to another man and some how or another all of this information was common knowledge in their community. S/he had never known the slightest bit of acceptance. Affirmation was alien. She was born black. Her mother named her *intentionally left blank* (I'm not making this up) but she preferred to be called *blank* or sometimes *blank again*.(lawyer advises to leave this blank for a host of reasons) She grew up in Hampton, Arkansas, which, to the best of my knowledge, isn't exactly known for being progressive or shall we say, tolerant of diversity. She is twenty-four years old and according to test taken at an Arkansas Adult Continuing Education Center at Lonoke, AR her education was at a second grade level. She could not even begin to count change back. She had no idea what geography even is much less where any place was. Her mother put her in foster care when she was eight years old and she was "Hot Potatoed" from one unhealthy home to another unhealthy home. She said that she had moved more times than she could count. She told me that my home was the only home where she actually felt acceptance. That made me feel good, but also very sad. When I met her she was sleeping under a bridge in the cold, in the rain. She had a companion and the two of them where equals in intelligence, only the companion had a little more education. He got that in prison. Her companion's name is *intentionally left blank*. His is a sad case as well. He had been beaten and abused by his mother and father. The only time when he felt security was when he was in prison. This caused him to be reluctant to leave prison. He had refused all rights to parole and he, of his own choosing, served every single day of a seven years sentence. He has severe Attention Deficit Disorder. I like him a lot. I kept both of them in my home for ten months or so. We managed to get him SSI Disability Income and they got themselves their own place down in the ghetto in North Little Rock. They moved out last Wednesday. I don't have much hope of them "making it" but I have done all that I can do. At least I think and hope that I have done all that I can do. God's protection has been requested.

Rumors

Why do people rumor?
I listen to c-span a lot
I'm kind of a news junky like that.
I sometimes like to listen to the call-ins.
I sometimes get a chuckle.
(I sometimes say I too much)
but anyway, people are funny.
They are like sheep and
they sometimes almost trample
themselves to death over some rumor.
Rumors are like snakes.
They should be avoided, and respected
in the same sense that you should respect snakes
or lightning, or handguns. Not in the sense that
one respects someone because of some noble character
such as courage, or generosity.
Respect in that you are aware of how it can harm and do
damage.
One rumor can do havoc like a hurricane can.
And people are funny like sheep.
Stand back and watch somebody throw a rumor in the mist.
(don't throw it yourself, someone could get hurt and you
would be liable)
People scatter in herds like stampeding cattle.
Swine flu is a good example.
The rumor goes " Somebody from Philadelphia
died from swine flu"
Holy Crap it killed somebody!
We are all going to die!
Let's get the hell out of here!
And off they go with their heads in a fuzz.
They'll settle down in a little while.

Suffice it to say, Rumors are not good.

ROSES ARE DEAD.

Roses are dead
violets are too
My world is dark and blue.
Because the hope and dream I almost had
is slowly dying too.
*

RIDGE CLIFF

On northern cliffs
An howling makes
On southern but an hiss
I am all but one with this
A murmur and a wish.

Ribeyes

^

It is enough.

It is enough for me,
it is enough for me for now,
to know that one of them is mine.

I'll take me mine;
all to myself.
Rhapsody;
sublime.

kent

*

REMNANTS

There in the cafe'
there in the theatre
there along the roadside
there along the river's bank
there beside the sea
here, there and everywhere
remnants of her and me.

REKINDLE

To have lost love
is a terrible curse.
To never have known it
is even worse.
If we are to survive
as this whole human race,
we must kindle the fire
with the warmth of embrace.
Else we'll leave this ole earth
no better a place,
just a glowing small ball
with lots of good space.

Purpose

What is purpose?
Is it the what of what something
was intended to do.
A hammer's purpose is to hit the head
of a nail and drive it in. Or also you can see clearly
the design has a head and a tail.
You can use a hammer to remove a nail.
It was designed that way.
It was designed specifically for that purpose.
If you try to screw a screw with a hammer,
you won't have much luck.
(luck is another matter, I don't know its purpose.)

I like to think of purpose.
It feels good when I'm aligned
with what I think my BIG purpose is;
My purpose here is love.

Puppet

I'm just her little puppet
and she has all my strings
she can make me jump
or make me cry
make me do all kinds of things.

I'm going to break these strings some day
I don't know what I'll do then
'cause everyone knows
that here in the real world
puppets don't have brains.

Public service

I'm going to be right there downtown again
right there on President Clinton Blvd.
right in the heart of The District
in the heart of The Market.

Right there across from the Main library
and the Arkansas Institute of Studies
or some nomer just the same
and the The Clinton School Of Public Service
the River Market Campus.

It seems to me that
the best way to be
of Public Service,
is to be a bee
of Public Service.

Which would be infinitely made easier
without carrying a tax of wax on my back, and legs.
How can one fly with a tax of wax attached?

But I'm meandering toward a big black hole of thought.
I'm sorry but it is almost April 15th.

I'm going to be living and working downtown again.
I like that Big City life—IIEEE!!
Where vendors and spenders
mingle and mangle and sometimes haggle
over the price of a ham
One of Arkansas's best.

I like people from far away places
I like to read their faces
The lines on faces are some of the best ever written

I'm excited about Downtown
Gonna bring the Ridge to the Rock.
I'm gonna Rock the Rock.
Don't talk the talk
—if you can't
Rock the Rock.
IIIIEEEEEE!!!!!!!!!

Prized Tattoos

She sported two black eyes
like prized tattoos.
Hit me again she said.
So I hit her hard across the face
with the back of my hand
careful not to hurt my knuckles
for I needed my hands to earn my living
and I still needed to put two sons through college.

Her head went back and blood splattered
through the air in slow motion.
A strange laughter escaped her lips.
She looked to be intoxicated.

Come on big boy, hit me like you mean it.
Don't hold back.
Don't worry about them pretty boy hands.
Hit me like this.

I didn't see it coming.
She slapped me hard across my face.
As a reflex, I hit her full fisted, as hard as I could.
Her head snapped back.
I heard bones crack.

I woke up startled to the phone ringing.
The ceiling fan spinning.
Hello, I said.
It was her.
What are you doing? Still asleep?
No, not now I said.
I made you some coffee.
It is nice and strong.
Come get you some.

I told her I'd be right over.
I threw on some clothes
hopped in the car
and headed towards her flat.
Wondering what it all meant.
If anything.

PRAYER FOR PRESIDENT OBAMA

Please!
Bless him, and protect him.
Bless him, and protect him.
Oh Lord, My God,
I pray.

PLANE CRASH.

I was trying to sleep,
but sometimes sleep just won't come.
It had not been a good day.
On top of that I was sick.
Tossing and turning, rechecking the alarm clock again and
again.
Was it the text msgs, the age, the fish sticks, the g.d.
goofiness?
I turned on the tube. There had been a plane crash near
Buffalo.
She was born in Buffalo and her mother lives there.
I tried to call. No answer.
I text, again. All of the sudden the previous problems that I
had
seemed so small. One man on TV lost his sister. He mentioned
her by name. His voice broke
I looked her up on the net. 24 years old. Single. Went to high
school in Clarence N.Y. right outside of Buffalo. That was
where the plane crashed. She was attending law school in
Jacksonville, Florida. Going home for the weekend. Going
home to die. Her Mother and Father were all the way down in
Florida . . . . On vacation. At this very minute they are in hell.
Bless their hearts. To lose a precious daughter. Maybe in her
sixth year
of higher education. What a major blow!
I'm sure I'll never get to sleep now.
Sleep seems trivial now.
My problems so trivial now.

Perspective

I can't see it
the way that you see me
all slothful
and scandalous
and deceiving.
I can't see it
the things that you imagine
that you see.
The things that you think
you see in me.
You say that I'm a liar
that I have been untrue.
You say that I'm unfaithful
a womanizer too.
But I just can't see it.
The me that you claim to see,
I just can see in me.

I think your vision
says more about you
than it says about me.

PERSPECTIVE

The chocolate syrup
had solidified
right there beside my head,
on the nightstand there beside my bed,

But not before it had captured pennies and other things
a match whose head was spent, an ant or two,
a nickel, and the end of some USB port-like thing,
and yes some bits of cracker too.

Oh some would see and say; "what a mess!"
me? I cried: "Eureka!"
"I've created art!"

Paranoria.

Paranoria
is a mean
little mind tricking machine,
that bores right down
to the ultimate truth.
That which he knows
without any proof.
Paranoia.
At the seat of the brain
it makes motives suspect
and magnifies weakness
as though it were bad.
Paranoia.
It twist the reality
to prisms of light
slightly tainted
and blurred
shifted red.
Paranoia.
Paranoia is mean
by day and by night
It'll trick you and tease you
while digging in tight.
Paranoia.

On Dating

One of the bad things
About writing
Is that you have
To date

And everyone
Will know
In retrospect
What you did.

And When.

Not This Time

did you hear me not
outside your window last night
did you hear me not throwing pebbles
the way that I use to do?

did you hear me not
outside in the cold
trying to get your attention
the way that I use to do?

did you hear me,
not outside your door?
That's good, because
I didn't hear me too.

Nostalgia

I know I'm taking my time
before moving on down the line.
I know I'm lingering,
there's something a simmering,
in this nostalgic and young man's mind.

NIGHT DREAMS

I've been spending my nights with you
the late night hours
the early morning hours too.

Just last night
we were along the beach.
Alone, there along the beach.
You were well within my reach
as we lay there in the sand.

The soft moonlight
and the salty mist
the rhythm of the tide
the rhythm of you and I.

Just as my hand touched you
I woke up
to this dirty room
the smell of cigarettes
empty cans
the radio playing some sad love song.

I've been spending my nights with you
the late hours
and the early morning hours too.
I've been spending my time with you
I've nothing better to do.

Necessities

There are many things
I can live without.
And toilet paper,
ain't one of them.

My specialty?

Me,
and Charity,
she is my niece,
we love each other,
with a pure love,
and we love our customers too.
We love a lot.
But in a very good way,
a pure way,
a way that is true.
How about you?

What is your specialty?

My Handiwork

These problems are of my making.
Therefore they can be of my fixing.

My Friend.

All I could deduce
was that he liked looking
over his shoulder.

He came to me all in a bind
and needing help.
He'd ignored a judge's order
and was facing serious jail time.

We went before the judge,
a friend of mine,
and explained
and ask for mercy.

The judge, my friend
weighed the facts
and partly, I think, on my behalf
was lenient on him.

He allocated fines
gave him months and month on end
and fully explained his distain
for being in the court's contempt.

My client was remorse
said he fully understood
and made the pledge.
Nothing else was said.
He would be prompt this time
as planned.

I saw him just today,
said he was behind again.
Why should I beg?
I went out on a limb,
out on a limb for him.

I should be more careful
with who is
and who isn't
my friend.

Maybe We're Winning!

I heard a statistic today
things may be going our way.
They said more people today were alive,
than all those who had ever died.
Which made me stop and think
that maybe there's a chance,
that we're winning the war on death.

May day, May day

Today is May Day!
Time for them military parades
time to line them fancy tanks up
the glorious missiles too
time to rally around the threat
with all them goose stepping troops.

Time to wake them leaders up
show them all what we can do
with an Heil Heil here
and an Hail Hail there
palm of the hand extended at forty-five degrees
"one for all and all for the state"-salute.

Today is May Day!
but now it is Two Thousand and Nine
May all that May Day stuff
be enshrined in some dark, swank,
and glorious tomb.

MAX

It is enough for me,
enough for now,
that Max needs me.
He is actually glad to see me
when I get home.
I know it is only for the food,
but food is what I do.
So I greet Max,
and Max greets me,
as friends are want to do,
und Er mir zum Hause welkommens.
Max thinks in German.
He is a Sheppard.
I am glad to see him;
he is glad to see me too.
The aroma of bacon
gives him a hint
that daddy is
about to feed me.
Add two parts water,
one part rice,
read the paper,
and let it rest.
Max is patient;
I am proud.
He knows that I am home.
Home from someplace;
only God knows where.

I let it steep,
then add some ice,
Max likes ice with his rice;
warm makes him sick.
I can't relate.
But, I'm glad for Max.
Selfish, I guess it is.
Cause it sure makes me feel good,
though it may not be what I had wished,
it is enough for me, enough for me for now,
to feel that I am needed.

Lucky

Told you I was lucky.
Didn't I tell you so?
You don't have to tell me.
I already know.

Love songs III

Love songs are like cigarettes.
I don't like to like them,
but like them I do.
.

Oh, I can quit them anytime.
It's the starting back,
that I can't seem to beat.

LOVE IS MORPHINE

Love is like morphine
it gives me the shits . . .
it makes me numb all over..
more than anywhere else.
I love love
I may be addicted.
*

LOOKING AND SPINNING

To the south is Louisiana.
She's good enough for me.
The cookin' makes up for any lack.
I get a kick out of her looking
like a bungled French boot.
You just know it's gotta hurt.
East is Mississippi
we share that delta dirt.
As rich as any land on earth
Made richer by black man's blood.
I love me some Mississippi,
she kept us from being last
in many a many thing.
To the west is Texas
To big to be defined.
(football excluded!)
As long as she stays there where she is
everything will be just fine.
But to the North
Is Misery
Damn her and her Compromise.
Might as well as been a Northerner
for all the help you were.
Oh, I'm not bitter,
I just don't like Misery.
Eureka Springs
is as North
as I ever
want
to be

*

LISTENING TO LOVE MUSIC

Our radio at The Shoppe
has been tuned to love songs lately.
Man, I've been missing out.
Every song I hear takes me back
It wakes me up.

"Amazed" by Lonestar.
"You Give Good Love" by Whitney
Hall and Oates, Toni Braxton, James Taylor.
All of them singing,
singing about love.

I love to love a lot
It makes the sunshine sunny
and pleasant,
not hot and overbearing,
but a faithful gentle friend
there to light the way.

I really like listening
to love music.

Lies

There are so many lies
That I have heard,
That we all have heard.
They almost become common place.
We just kind of accept them
As a common form of everyday conversation.
It isn't hard to read between the lines
And hear just what it is that someone is selling.
People call me all the time and tell me how
They want to help me.
People in Bangkok, or India, or San Francisco,
They call me. And they want to help me.
They want to save me money and make my life easier;
They want to make my life better, because I'm good
And I've got a good track record
And they can look at numbers and they can tell that I work hard.
People come into the Shoppe and ask for me.
Not necessarily by name; But they ask for the manager in charge.
I stop whatever work I am doing and I come to see who is calling.
So often, I'm inclined to say always,
They give me their name, or a name that they claim
It makes no difference to me.
They've been shopping with me for years, they claim
I've always treated them good, they claim.
And they've got this little situation
Just down the road a piece: They need a little gas
Just need a little cash, maybe to fix a flat
Or some food to feed the kids.
(not food exactly, cash would do just nicely)
I ask this stranger, whom I've never seen
Just what it is they need?
They usually ask for Ten

Or sometimes even Twenty.
Little do they know they could have said a Hundred.
They don't realize that I know that they are my brother.
So many lies that I have heard.
I ponder what is the most common.
I love you?
The check is in the mail?
To be honest with you?
(That is a red flag for certain)
I've come to the conclusion
That the most common lie that I have heard is:
I would never lie to you.

LAH-LAH LAND

there where it is that we do not need
with the jum-dee-jer and the jum-der-dee
cavort and frolic 'neath the jum-yum tree
I wanna go back to the dum-lier sea
just my dum-lier bride and my dum-lier me
and sip from the brac-lean cup my brac-leon tea
and listen to the waves and sleep the sweet sleep
and let the con-glomeon sand
slip through my con—gloveon hands
and watch my dum-lier mate scour sour and weep weep.

KNOWLEDGE

KNOWLEDGE
KNOWLEDGE
EVERYWHERE
AND NOT A THOUGHT
OF WISDOM THUNK.

Knowing What I Have Known

It isn't that I didn't know.
It is not like I still don't know.
Not that I haven't known;

Not that I haven't seen.
For I have seen
for a long-long time.

I could see it in her eyes
the first moments when she would awaken
and her eyes would first meet mine.

It was there
so plain to see,
the disappointment,
the sorrow,
the regret.

Anything but love.
Everything but me.

JOUST

We joust about
like little boats
on choppy seas.

Bailing water
from left to right
trying not to sink.

It is enough

It is enough for me
enough for me for now
to feel the hot sun beat down on me.
It is enough for me
enough for me for now
to know that I'm alive.
To feel the hot sun,
to know and feel the struggle,
to know that my father felt
this self same sun
beat down upon his brow
to know that he too struggled
as I struggle.
I and my Father are one.
But he is gone
and it is for me now
to feel the heat
to know the strain.
It is enough for me
enough for me now,
My moment in the sun.

ILLUSIONS

Soft as a summer breeze
these heartfelt dreams of mine.
And all I have
and all I've lost
were never even mine.

I WONDER.

I wonder sometimes
if there is any way
that she could see some goodness in me.
If maybe I provided
a nice place to live
and built a fence
and put the good carpet down
and painted the room
and paid for the roof
and did my best to fix the water heater
as feebly as my best might have been.

and hired a good dentist
and fixed the rest
and life insurance
health insurance, 529-F's
groceries galore
and did back-flip somersaults
and sit and smiled
and chit and chatted
I wonder if
that would have made
a difference.

I can't really wonder.
I know the truth.
The answer is:
Of course not.

I WONDER.

I wonder if
she thinks of me
like I don't
think of her.

I Wish That I Could Call..

I'd like to be able to call
and just say: Happy Birthday!
I hope you have a Happy Birthday.
but I can't do that.
It's not that simple.
Nothing is simple.

It always gets complicated
like when in simple conversation
I lamented that I was out of cigarettes.
That was it.
A simple lament.
and a jovial request.
"Why don't you bring me some?"
Nothing more,
Nothing less.

I had had a shot of Brandy
the liquid kind
and I couldn't drive.
I'd swore an oath unto myself.
If I'd had a drink, I wouldn't drive.

Why don't you bring me a cigarette?
I asked.
Are you serious? was her reply.
Sure, I guess . . . . Why not?
I could use a smoke.
She said she'd be right there.

Wow! I was blown away.
She was going to do something nice for me.
And she did just that.

We sat and chit and chatted.
It really was quite good.
I was glad to see her and glad for her to see my room.
It was nothing more than that.

Very simple.
Very easy.
I slept good that night
and was thankful for the dialogue.

But later on
when the truth came out
the truth as she perceived it,
which really spoke volumes,
not of truth,
but of perceptions.

She spoke of her magnanimous generosity,
and used for her example,
the other night when I was too drunk to drive
and so she, in her magnanimous mercy, brought me cigarettes.

Forgive me here my language
but in my defense
I'm immersed in frustration.

Shit, damn, hell, blank.
Something so precious,
so simple,
so easy,
was a blankety blank, mother-blank-ing example
of my frustration. What the blanking hell!!!

I wish that I could call,
Just to say; Happy Birthday!
but you see.
I can't.

I Think My World Into Existence.

A man is the sum total of his own thoughts
the trick is to think properly
accurately, honestly.

The trick is to learn to desire
that which is worth desiring.

And to be content
with that which is.

To be, or not to be.
That is the question.
that is ask of thee.

It may not be original
but it is no less true.
It's the root of all you think.
The catalyst of what you do.
Therefore the source of happiness
or the seat of discontent.
It's all in how you think.

So try to think properly.
Desire good things.
They will come to you.
There is no way that they will not
if you will but think and do (work) properly.

I Have Become
The Not Me

And it's starting to bother me. I'm not the me I was.
Not even close to the me that I had dreamed
I am weak and emasculated, ineffectual
just wasting
perfectly good air.

Hole In My Heart

You put a hole in my heart, honey.
That's the place where the love used to grow.
Now there's no laughter,
now there's no sunshine,
and this heartache of mine
just won't leave me alone.
You said that we were in Love.
You said we were more than just friends.
Said we were lovers
meant for each other,
said that it never would end.
But somebody else came along,
and gave you a dance and a song.
You went Away!
Didn't even say: Good-bye, Good-luck, or So-Long.
And you put a hole in my heart, honey.
That's the place where the love used to grow.
Now there's no laughter,
now there's no sunshine,
and this heartache of mine,
just won't leave me alone.
Tears roll down my face
onto my pillow each night,
And your memories, they haunt me all day,
'cause the love we used to share
you now share with someone else
and that image, it burns in my mind.
And you put a hole in my heart, honey.
That's the place where the love used to grow.
Now there's no laughter,
and now there's no sunshine,
and this heartache of mine,
it just won't leave me a lone.

HEAVY.

I don't want to be heavy.

I just want to be light
so I can fly
not fly away, just fly
way up high
like a goldfish in the sky.
Wouldn't that be something?

So won't you,
come away with me?
We can fly together
and soar
like two whor . . . . horses,
Wouldn't that be something two?

Then instead of being Pegasus
We could be Pegasi
Way up in the sky
together—you and I.
Wouldn't that be something three?

Healer.

The laying on of hands
may be the best healer
of all time
and eternity.

It doesn't have to
be love
but it helps
to the extreme.

Head and Soul

Like is of the head.
Love is of the soul.
To love unconditionally
is to know
to be whole.

HATE IT WHEN I HATE

I hate to admit that I hate.
But when love goes to pulling
and making me think
I could put this all together
into a nice little box called me.
I hate it when I think . . .
I could do that too.

HAPPY.

I love communication
one on one.
Just speaking freely,
on whatever we want.

I love touching gently
let harshness be damned.
I love being with you,
happy with who I am.

Gone For Good.

I'm telling you now
if I leave you again
I ain't coming back.
I'm serious this time.
I mean it.
If I walk out that door,
I'll be gone for good this time.
Listen to me.
I'm saying, If I go . . .
there ain't no coming back.
I'll be gone this time for good.
I can see you don't believe me
so I'm telling you now
I'll be gone for good this time.
Don't you know I mean it?
I'm fixing to walk out for good.
You don't want me to leave, this time
'cause I'm telling you
if I go this time I ain't coming back.
What the hell are handing me?
You know I ain't taking my hat!

GEMINI-PART II

There is a king that resides somewhere in me
He is a noble king
the kind of king
that I'd like to be
if I had a kingdom for a day.

There is a pauper somewhere inside of me
He is a poor old pauper too.
No plan or land
his palm up hand
I wish he would run away.

Funny

The last poem I had written
(it was just this morning)
I said that people are funny.

Tonight she said I was funny.
It made me feel funny.
funny is a funny word.
sometimes it means funny, haha funny.
Like a comedian is funny.
Sometimes it means funny, strange funny.
Like an odd thing is funny.

I don't know a person in this world
who laughs when they hit their funny bone.
Maybe it is the humorous bone
like the femur bone.
I just don't know.
I don't feel so funny anymore.
Unless by funny you mean odd or peculiar,
then I do feel funny.

Like the last kid picked to play kickball.
One team was going to be stuck with me.
I was the odd man out and everyone agreed
that I had to go somewhere.
No one ever said: Yeah, he's on our team.

They knew I couldn't kick.
So who would want to pick?
That always made me feel funny.
I always feel funny.
That kind of funny.

FUNNY BONE

It is kind of funny
but not ha-ha funny
when we see ourselves
like others see us
and the images leap
from no place known
images alien
foreign
obtuse
not at all like me
but I see for a minute
what they think of me.
Not a whole lot unlike
hitting your funny bone,
only worse.
More like,
having your breath knocked out of you.

FORGIVE ME.

If I curse too loudly,
please,
forgive me.
My heart is black,
My mind confused.
I don't mean to be ugly,
I don't mean to be rude.

FIDDLE STICKS

Where I come from,
from my neck of the woods,
out there in the sticks,
it is better to be played like a fiddle
than a sissy violin.

FDNH

I like that
First Do No Harm
When you don't know how to respond
First do no harm.
When planning the day
FDNH
When frustration
Leaps up in your face
Like a wild wooly buger
Hiding in the bushes
FDNH
When you want to smack the living blank
Out of your blankety blank blank stupid assed blank
FDNH
And even when you would unleash that tongue
and let your verbal mortars fly
tossing little lethal hand grenades of venomous words
Viseral, Vitriolic, Eruptions.
FDNH
And even unto yourself
When you look into that mirror
And even though you may want to tell yourself
That you were right to do wrong
And pamper your pride
Keep in mind
That it is harmful to be deceptive
First Do No Harm!

Fairy tales

It is only in fairy tales
that they live—happily ever after.
Here in the real world
they always die in
The End.

.

Everything Is Gonna Be Fine.

I ain't telling you what I know
I'm telling you what I think
and I think everything is gonna be fine.

I know the road is full of holes
and bumps and dinks abound
It ain't always gonna be easy
what fun would that be?
Sometimes its gonna be tough.

But the tough will make the tender
so much more of a splendor
that the tough will be just fine too
and if I bite off more than I can chew
I'll just chew, chew, and then chew

I ain't telling you what I know
I'm telling you what I think
and I think everything is gonna be fine.

EVERYDAY..

Everyday
is always a making
every pattern
of the brain.

ENDLESS REPETITION

over and over again
the earth moves down
to the core and is pushed up
as molten lava to the top
and soon solidifies
as a mountain chain
where green grass grows
where birds fly
where insects die
where I
am an endless repetition too.
Not some far off distant kingdom
after death.
But here and now
with hopes and dreams
then hot regret.

Emma

It's hard to think
Nineteen Spring-times
Have graced your grave.

Emma Joelle

Yellow dress so cute
tiny hands, my fingernails
forever gone
I ache for thee.

Earth To Kent

You can no longer just be dead weight,
either start bailing water
or start swimming.

Hello, Hello
Earth to kent.

DON'T TOUCH ME THERE

It isn't fair.
Don't touch me there
touch my body
touch my mind
touch my soul
touch me anywhere
anywhere you want
but please
Don't touch me there
leave my heart alone.

DON'T TAKE THIS BET.

I'm not sure where I'm going
but I'm pretty sure I'm not going to get there.
But if I do, I bet I'm late
and I bet I won't know where I am
once I get there.
*

Doctor

It's gonna take a doctor
to make me right again.
Gonna take some kind of doctor
to make me whole again.
It's gonna take some kind of prescription
something really good
to make me laugh
and make me smile
to make me me again.
Maybe some kind of witch doctor
to do the mumble-jumble
and do some kind of wild dancing thing
maybe mix some kind of potions
maybe pull some kind of strings.
but it is gonna take some kind of doctor
some kind of doctor good
to make me me
and make me smile
to make me me again.

Dixie

These shards of glass, go broken,
like daze gone buy.

Look Away!
Look Away!
Look Away, Dixie Land.

DECISIONS, DECISIONS

The Golden Rule: Act in a way you would want others to act toward you.

The Utilitarian Principle: Act in a way that results in the greatest good for the greatest number.

Kant's Categorical Imperative: Act in such a way that the action taken under the circumstances could be a universal law or a rule of behavior.

The Professional Ethic: Take actions that would be viewed as proper by a disinterested panel of professional peers.

The TV Test: Always ask, "Would I feel comfortable explaining to a national TV audience why I took this action?"

The Legal Test: Ask whether the proposed action or decision is legal. Established laws are generally considered minimum standards for ethics.

The Four-Way Test: Ask whether you can answer "yes" to the following questions as they relate to the decision: Is the decision truthful? Is it fair to all concerned? Will it build goodwill and better friendships? Will it be beneficial to all concerned?

Always Remember: Everything that you know you learned from somewhere. Therefore; the profuse proclamation of disclaimers is nothing more than perfunctory displays of pompous digression, edifying nothing.

Disclaimer: Portions of the preceding were excerpted from (and thereafter edited by me) Wikipedia.

Death.

What is wrong with death?
I mean, it is inevitable.
And whether or not it is today
or tomorrow,
or if by some strange
inexplicable chance
a hundred years from now,
still it is coming pretty damned quick.
Then what?
Who knows?
I don't think this . . . .
That we'll walk on streets of gold
or get seventy fresh virgins
or writhe in unquenchable fire
from can to can't
and there ain't no can't.

I really don't think I'll even think.
But the now I have.
And now I do.
And now is really all I have.
and all the things I think,
are manifest in what I do.

So this I know . . . .
I think.
therefore I'm Am,
Therefore I am not dead
therefore I can do do
shit.

DARKNESS

The universe is more dark than anything.
This half glimmering ball called Earth
is an anomaly.
And the glare that covers the darkness
in the daytime
is an optical illusion
on the other side is dark
complete empty darkness.
Much like my heart.
The light chases the dark away
and hides the stars
but they are there
I know they are there
still shimmering
in the dark.

Dark Blue Wind

Black is back to me again
dark whirls of thought against the wind
and all the hopes I thought I knew
blew out the door with wishes too.

Subtle are the memories
ephemeral are the dreams in me
and all my longings are of the past
my ambitions too are dead at last.

Where hath all the laughter gone
the merriment and lighter song
for I am but a shell of me
a hollow core, blank destiny.

The younger me that thought he knew
The stronger me has vanished too
the darker me is here again
the wind is blowing blue again.

Curiosity

They say that curiosity
killed the cat.
I wonder why.

CHOICES.

I know a little about love
even more do I know of sad.
And if forced to choose
between the two,
I'd choose Love
It ain't half as bad.

CAVEAT

I accept them all with caveat
I accept that they are human,
I accept that humans are fragile,
flawed,
glorious,
week
and strong
all at once,
in a word Divine-
Human
all at once.

I accept them all with caveat,
excepting only
I can NOT accept judgmental.

CATCHING UP

Catching up
shan't take longer
than the event
caught up
on.

BROADWAY PLAY.

I've got a Broadway Play
all written
inside my head.
What a beautiful ensemble.

Oh, Dixie! Oh, Dixie!
How much longer
can you hold on?
I can see it all
inside my head.

BOB COX

If I am to other people
as Bob Cox has been to me,

Then I will always be to others:
Kind and patient,
Gentle and long-suffering,
Generous and caring,
Understanding and helpful.

If they ask for a mile
I'll give them two.
If they want my shirt,
They can have my coat too.

If their cart gets stuck,
I'll get out and push,
(Never mind the pain)
I'll tell them that better days are just down the road a piece,
right around the next corner there,
tell them I sent you, and they'll take you in.

If I am to others,
as Bob Cox has been to me,
I'll be planting some pretty good seeds.
And what it means to be a Christian
will be something that can be seen,
(as opposed to only heard)
Bob Cox has been
a friend to me.

Bi-polar Nation.

I live in a bi-polar nation
It really gets hard to understand it
Unless you have a bi-polar filter
like I do.

With one breath they say:
I thank God that I love Him So.
I thank God That I Know him so
much better than anybody else.

With the next breath they say:
Round them up and send them back down south,
they got no business here in My land.
Who do they think they are?
Pursuing Life, Liberty and Happiness like that.
Send them back!
Send them Back!

Whenever I hear these bi-polar claims
My filter filters it out.
Bigots need Love too.
They can't help it, They are Ignorant,
and Hypocrites.

I know that sounds harsh
But listen to John
Who walked with Jesus
Who was known as the disciple that Jesus loved
John the Beloved.

He said, and I quote: If any man says that he loves God,
but he hates his brother. That man is a LIAR!
(emphasis mine)
And the truth is not in him. unquote.

That Mexican Friend of mine is My Brother.
And quite frankly it chaffs me to listen to
your bi-polar, bigoted, ignorant, hypocritical, lying self.
So sit down and shut the hell up!

BAD

Oh, I can be bad
all by myself
that isn't hard to do.
But to do good
really good
I need a comforting soul.
I can do bad all by myself
and run the streets 'till dawn
and drink away the afternoon
and piddle around and yawn.
But if I want to do good
really good
I cannot go it alone.
Bad, I can be bad without company.
It is an easy thing for me,
but if I want to do good
really do good
I need my house a home.
I don't want to do bad,
I really don't.
I want to do good.
I want to give my heart and soul away
to that lovely one that comforts me,
that believes in me,
that sees good it me,
that keeps me from being alone.

AWAKENING TO SLEEP.

Seeing but not with eyes
Knowing but did not know
Here but not quite hearing
Dead but not yet gone.

ART

Art
That is what it was to me.
Art
Lives scrapped out
with a dull knife.
There along the river's bank.
With scrabbles of rubble
and pieces of fabric
wadded up
to make a pillow.
Artist.
"You're an artist", I said.
All of this
The river
The pillow
You
This is Art.
His eyes welled up like the river
that boiled like soiled blood.
"Fuck You Man!
This ain't no goddamned Art.
This is me!
And this shit is hard.
Sit in your goddamned self
and call this . . . Art?
Fuck you man.
And your art-shit self."

ARLINGTON

Headstones Erect
Saluting me
At Arlington.

APRIL 20 2009

Happy Birthday Emma!
Miss You! See You Soon!
Happy Birthday Hitler!
Good Riddance! Go to Hell!
You Bastard.

Amendment

We need an amendment to the U.S. Constitution.
Not to change it, I think, but to clarify what it already says.
The Founding Fathers were very clear
about who has the power to Declare War.
That power is fully vested in The U.S. Congress.
The Congress should not be able to abdicate that
responsibility
and bequeath it to The President as if it were a gift.
The President has the responsibility to execute, or prosecute,
a war.
The President is, at all times, Commander-in-Chief.
Congress alone has the capacity to—Declare War.
The President can not, legally, declare war any more than he
can judge a law. It isn't within the perimeters of his or her
office.
And Congress should not be able to toss that responsibility
like a hot potato to The President any more than The
Judiciary can abdicate responsibility for interpreting laws.

It was reasonably determined that it should take an Act of
Congress
for the United Stated of America to be muddied by the awful
necessity of War. It was a strategic, vital, element of what we
call Checks and Balances. It would require a Group of Men,
rather than One Man to Declare War. This was one of the clear
lines of delineation from England and King George. Without
that Declaration, it could be reasonable argued that there
should be no engagement. It should be illegal, I think, for the
United States to be involved in a war which has not been
declared by the U.S.Congress.

For further illumination read The U.S. Constitution; Article
One, Section Eight, and The Federalist Papers number
Sixty-Nine and number Twenty-Four. I feel strongly about this.
No single person should have the prerogative, nor
responsibility
of putting our troops in harms way.
But if We, As a People, deliberately reason otherwise, than
we should change The U.S. Constitution, with an Amendment.
Kent

ALL THAT MATTERED.

It didn't really matter
what was said.
he measured everything by laughter.

If there was laughter he probed
and prodded a little farther.
That was all that mattered
was that there was laughter.
*

ALL SYSTEMS ARE GO . . . .
ALMOST.

All systems looking go
It's looking check for liftoff
All systems looking go.

Just a small faint sound of fuzz
about days gone past
and things I can't control
Not enough to warrant
stopping such a terrific launch.

Don't scrub this launch
I'm ready
All systems they are go.
I want to go in orbit,
more than
you'll ever know.

Aiming high.

Often times when the moon comes up
I take my rifle and sight it in
And chase that man across the sky
aiming for his right smug eye.

Half the time I can see the next night
places where I've nicked him good
and I fire away and make him run
each night a little more damage done.

But when he's had enough of me
no dead-eye shooting or chivalry
Can stop that moon from bowing up
until he gets full faced and sometimes red.

And I start to fear for my life
and I take dead aim, not once nor twice
but I fire at will and watch him run
we go back and forth
from month to month.

I think that maybe sometime soon
I'll wear out that quarrelsome moon
My experience and wisdom will get the best of him
then I'll take on his next of kin.
I'll need a bigger gun.

ACQUAINTED

I have been one acquainted
with the dark and the blues.
I have felt the loneliness
of being alone
of being an outcast
within my own home.

I've been the subject
of false accusations
but found comfort within myself
of knowing the truth.

I've held my tongue
when I could have spoken the truth
and laid my accusers low.

I've kept my own counsel
not sinking below
the depths of their cunning
and losing my soul.

I've done wrong
(no doubt about that)
but I've often done right too.

And if only I know.
Than that is more than enough.
Here in the Night.

A Storm II

Something there is about a storm
that makes me want to know it.
I like to feel a storm
deep within my bones
inside my heart
deep within my head
deep inside of me.

I am one with this world.
and a storm is just a reflection
of my life
a reflection of me.

I here the rumble
beyond the ridge
and I can gauge
by the wind
about just when
I'll be in the midst
of the storm.

I can usually get pretty close
I sometimes set my watch
and wait and watch.

As the trees begin to bobble up and down
like an audience gives a standing ovation
they bid almage to the king.
Up and down they wave
and the wind blows
and soon the drops begin to fall.
The heavy bass and rumble of thunder
like an orchestra on perfect cue
lets me know that my timing is good.

I often hear a silence
as the center approaches
and I wonder why I'm not afraid
as normal men would be
I'm different but I'm the same as others.
I'm ready to go if need be.

Soon great big drops of rain fall.
They remind me of thought.
As they splatter against the tin roof
just a little more proof
that my timing is good.

The storm passes over head.
I'm in the midst,
nice to know my watch is right.
My hair it stands on end
blowing in the wind..
It is all so . . . . electric.

A Lot Of Times

A lot of times
I ask myself,
what were you thinking?

A lot of times I just don't know.
But during those years-
those twelve plus years-
I was thinking-
and I know-
what I was thinking.

I was thinking-
like a kid:
"what did you do wrong?
was it something that you said?

Did you see that empty look
deep inside her eyes
this morning?
Did you see the way she felt,
she talked-
she walked-
she thought?"

"Yes, yes" I said.
I've seen it all along.
thinking so silent . . . .
unto myself,

—What did I do wrong?

A LONG TIME

It has taken me a long time
just to get here.
Just to get here,
where I can breath,
and feel,
and be me again.

It has taken me a long time
just to get here,
and it is only here
that I am.

But I am here.
And I am glad to be here.
But damn it has taken
a long time
just to,
get here.

Edwards Brothers Malloy
Oxnard, CA USA
December 29, 2014